MORE PRAISE FOR THIS BOOK

"*Becoming A Can Do Leader* provides specific suggestions and compelling examples to help leaders find the 'can-do zone'—an optimum mix of engagement and delegation that releases a team's energy in the most productive way."

—*Clay Jones, Retired Chairman and CEO, Rockwell Collins*

"*Becoming a Can-Do Leader* not only recognizes the struggles we all have as working managers, but gives practical tips for becoming more effective and efficient—a win-win all around!"

—*Karen Freedman, VP of Learning, global insurance company*

"A real break from the traditional 'play your position' leadership philosophy, *Becoming a Can-Do Leader* shows the reader how to lead and do at the same time, a valuable and necessary skill in today's fast-paced world."

—*Jane Brown Grimes, Former President and Chairman of the Board, U.S. Tennis Association*

"The new economy is demanding a new kind of leader who is both manager and technical expert—both leader and doer. Unfortunately there was precious little advice on how to effectively perform both roles, until now. *Becoming A Can-Do Leader* provides practical advice on mastering both roles, and creating a powerful learning culture."

—*Walter McFarland, Co-Author,* Choosing Change

"At Johnson & Wales University we like to disrupt conventional thinking in ways that will enable our students to continue to achieve professional success as leaders in the fast-changing world ahead. *Becoming a Can-Do Leader* provides practical steps for doing just that."

—*Thomas L. Dwyer, Provost, Johnson & Wales University*

"Unleashing the 'can-do' in each of us is a prerequisite for delivering value in today's workplace environments. *Becoming a Can-Do Leader* provides useful tips and tools so managers can deal with fast-moving change while still delivering on their commitments."

—*Beth Nelson Cliff, VP, Head of Talent and Organizational Development, Shire*

"*Becoming a Can-Do Leader* is a must read for those of us driven to distraction by having to be both a leader and a doer."

—*Tom Casey, Managing Principal, Discussion Partners Collaborative*

"*Becoming a Can-Do Leader* addresses the dichotomous relationship between leading and doing in a practical way that empowers managers to still do what they love while also building team capability. The can-do leadership approach offers a shift in leadership practices that is timely in the faster-paced, results-oriented world of business today."

> —*David J. DeFilippo, EdD, Chief Learning Officer, Suffolk Construction*

"Incorporating the can-do leader concepts and strategies into our management training has brought about a very positive measurable impact on the performance of our leaders and their teams."

> —*Don Nusser, VP and Manager of Learning & Development, Mott MacDonald North America*

"*Becoming a Can-Do Leader* stands out as a great how-to guide for those busy executives who both lead by doing and do by leading. I found it chock-full of useful insights and practical ideas and I'll keep it on my desk for daily use."

> —*Bill Wray, Chief Risk Officer, Washington Trust Bank*

"Based on real-world practical experience, *Becoming a Can-Do Leader* is a valuable resource for getting things done. The strategies, tools, and learning culture presented in this quick read are valuable for all managers."

> —*Paul R. Sullivan, Founder and former Managing Director, Global Partners Inc.*

"*Becoming a Can Do Leader* employs practical solutions to problems from a variety of fields that reach beyond the particular context, putting theory into practice, addressing challenges drawn from real life. The book's authentic distillation of complex strategies is a gift for player-managers in the new millennium."

> —*Emmett P. Tracy, MBA, PhD, Postgraduate Dean, Hult International Business School*

"The authors help managers become better leaders by providing useful ways to both develop their people and apply their professional expertise. A must read for managers at any level."

> —*Alan Frohman, Executive Coach Author, The Middle Manager's Challenge*

"In a time when managers are being asked to do more and more, *Becoming a Can-Do Leader* provides them with practical methods to get the work done, develop their people, and continue to grow professionally. It can turn a frustrated manager into a fulfilled one."

> —*Matt Nash, SVP Marketing, national donor advised fund charity*

BECOMING A
CAN-DO
LEADER

A GUIDE FOR THE
BUSY MANAGER

FRANK SATTERTHWAITE AND JAMIE MILLARD

PRESS

Frank Satterthwaite's author photo courtesy of Heidi Gumula.

The Can-Do Spirit VITALS Checkup and Can-Do Leader TPL Leadership Style Profiler in appendix I and II, respectively, are adapted from Dimensional Leadership, LLC and Lexington Leadership Partners, LLC.

ATD Press is an internationally renowned source of insightful and practical information on talent development, workplace learning, and professional development.

ATD Press
1640 King Street
Alexandria, VA 22314 USA

Ordering information: Books published by ATD Press can be purchased by visiting ATD's website at www.td.org/books or by calling 800.628.2783 or 703.683.8100.

Library of Congress Control Number: 2016954228

ISBN-10: 1-56286-992-2
ISBN-13: 978-1-56286-992-2
e-ISBN: 978-1-60728-117-7

ATD Press Editorial Staff
Director: Kristine Luecker
Manager: Christian Green
Community of Practice Manager, Management: Ryan Changcoco
Developmental Editor: Kathryn Stafford
Senior Associate Editor: Melissa Jones
Text Design: Iris Sanchez
Cover Design: Faceout Studio, Tim Green

Printed by Versa Press Inc., East Peoria, IL

Dedicated to our mothers, Emily Satterthwaite and Betty Millard, who brought us up to think can-do!

CONTENTS

ACKNOWLEDGMENTS

We would like to offer particular thanks to the following people and organizations for their contributions to our book.

Frank would like to thank:

- Johnson & Wales University for giving me the opportunity to experience what it is like to be a player-manager during my two-year stint as a professor in and director of their MBA program. And for giving me the encouragement to develop MBA courses based on the think TPL and VITALS checkup leadership models, which have evolved with Jamie's help into key strategies for converting player-managers into can-do leaders.

- I also want to thank my MBA students who have jobs as player-managers for providing me with feedback on how they have used the think TPL and VITALS checkup strategies in their own careers.

- I am particularly indebted to Everett Zurlinden who, as a lead engineer at a Fortune 500 corporation, helped me develop early versions of the think TPL model and profiler.

- And above all I want to thank my wife, Martha Werenfels. I have to admit that when I handed her the draft for our final chapter on how player-managers can become can-do champions, I did so with some trepidation. I was concerned because I knew that my wife, who is a partner in a highly successful Providence architecture firm, is a prime example of a player-manager who has become a high-profile can-do champion by using many of the strategies we highlighted in that chapter of our book. What a relief when she nodded her approval! She's also, I'd like to add, a champion wife and mom!

Jamie would like to thank:

- The U.S. Army, starting with my leadership experience as a West Point cadet and Army Ranger, and continuing with my tours of duty, which allowed me to experience firsthand the impact that can-do leaders have on unleashing the can-do spirit in others.

- The management consulting, executive coaching, and leadership training firms I have been fortunate to be part of, including KPMG and PwC (two of the Big 4, where I learned the intricacies of project management and re-engineering); CSC Consulting (where I helped global organizations manage large, complex organizational change); and especially Harbridge House (where I began my journey developing leaders worldwide at a variety of Fortune 100 companies across multiple industries).

- The many clients I worked with earlier in my career that gave me invaluable experiences in developing leaders, including Bayer MaterialScience, Draper Labs, DuPont, GE, IBM, PwC, Raytheon, Rockwell Collins, Rohm & Haas, Schering Plough, and the U.S. Navy.

- In particular, my more recent clients who have allowed me access to their leaders to test and refine many of the can-do leader concepts in this book, including Conti, EMC, KVH, Mott MacDonald, Nuance, VCE, and WEA Trust.

- The relationships I have enjoyed as a member of the Duke Corporate Education Global Educator Network; as an adjunct executive professor at Northeastern University; and as a professor at Hult International Business School.

- The late W. Edwards Deming, under whom I studied and applied his techniques at organizations like GE, Rohm & Haas Company, and Ford Motor Company. Deming taught me to challenge conventional thinking about the role of executives in shaping the organizational culture, processes, and systems of successful organizations.

- The numerous relationships with busy managers who were the basis of the many anecdotes and stories in the book. I've disguised your names and situations a bit to protect your identity, but you know who you are, and I thank you. These cameos and anecdotes are provided not as scientific proof of the validity of our findings, but to illustrate how our concepts and strategies can be effectively used by player-managers on the job. We leave it to the readers of this book to decide for themselves how useful these can-do leader strategies can be for them—by giving them a try!

- My business partner and co-founder of Lexington Leadership Partners, Gus Murby, for his lifelong friendship, ongoing support, keen insights, and early help in developing and coining the term *purposeful multi-impacting*. Together, as the "Gus and Jamie show," we continue to have a blast advising, engaging, developing, and often entertaining our clients with our Frick and Frack antics. We are united in the goal to help our clients achieve true business impact.

- And most important, there's my true inspiration—my very patient, understanding, and encouraging wife and best friend, Ann, who is an awe-inspiring mom, co-owner of an exceptional early learning center, and also very much a can-do leader in her business and in her life! I look forward to continuing to share the can-do spirit with you!

Jamie and Frank would both like to thank:

- The Association for Talent Development for giving us the opportunity to meet each other in local chapter meetings, and for helping us test and refine our can-do leader concepts in ATD blogs, conferences, and other forums. It's an honor to continue working with you to support the talent development profession.

- And, we would like to thank the supportive can-do staff at ATD, with extra kudos to our insightful editors Kathryn Stafford and Melissa Jones. And a special thanks to Ryan Changcoco, who kept us all on track throughout the process of publishing and promoting a new book with new ideas. You are, indeed, can-do champions!

INTRODUCTION: TOO BUSY TO READ THIS BOOK?

Do you feel too busy to read this book because you are a manager who also continues to do hands-on work? We're with you! And we would be happy to show you how you can start getting a lot more done—both as a leader and as an expert in your field—and feel better about the situation you are in as a manager and as a professional.

We'll give you some strategies you can put to work immediately. So that, contrary to popular belief, you will discover that as a can-do leader you can:

- Become a more effective manager by selectively doing professional work with the people who report to you.
- Continue to grow professionally in your area of specialization while you are also a manager.
- Find the time to be successful at both leading your team and practicing your specialty.
- Attain a higher level of professional distinction and employability by taking on management responsibilities while continuing to do professional work.

But first you have to let go of conventional management thinking by making the can-do mind shift. We invite you to read on to see how to make this transformation to become a can-do leader. We'll be right there with you every step of the way.

A Can-Do Leader: What's With This Name?

Becoming a can-do leader sounds good, but this book is about much more than just being the kind of manager who can get things done. Of course, in every chapter we'll share with you proven strategies for doing just that. But what we really want to show you is how to get things done in what has become a very difficult situation for many managers—having to be highly competent as both a leader and a doer—and to enjoy doing it.

If you find yourself saddled with leader-doer responsibilities and are not sure how best to proceed, you are most assuredly not alone. Today's knowledge-driven, cost-competitive work world is changing the way management gets done. People in management roles are increasingly being asked, told, or forced to be player-managers—hands-on leaders, who in addition to having formal management responsibilities, also continue to perform significant chunks of professional work that requires considerable technical-functional knowledge and skills.

This is happening because many organizations can no longer afford to promote their best talent to the leadership ranks and then allow them to focus exclusively on being managers. Their superior technical-functional skills, which typically take a long time to develop, are still very much needed for solving complex problems. And there's the danger that if they do not continue to do some hands-on work when they become managers, they will no longer have the knowledge they need to inform their management decisions.

There's also the brute fact that given the sharp focus these days on finding ways to cut costs, managers often find themselves expected to get the same volume of work done with fewer people. This translates to short-handed managers having to roll up their sleeves and do some of the work they would have liked to delegate. Like it or not, they, too, are becoming player-managers.

While the need for managers who are successful as both leaders and doers is very real today, this need is only likely to increase in the future. This translates to a really great career opportunity for both getting and keeping jobs throughout your career and becoming a star in your field. However, gaining a career edge will only happen if you know how to become an effective player-manager.

And that's where the trouble is. Management thinking hasn't properly caught up with the player-manager phenomenon. There are few solid guidelines available to help player-manager practitioners. Further complicating the matter is conventional management thinking, which suggests that leaders who get involved in actually doing the work are not being effective as managers. This thinking is not helpful, not realistic, and particularly counterproductive for people who find themselves in player-manager roles.

If you are struggling with how best to proceed as a player-manager, you are not alone. Many others in a similar role are having similar difficulties. Fortunately, we're here to help you. We know from personal experience the pressures felt by incumbents of the player-manager dual role: Frank in an academic setting, functioning simultaneously for several years as both a professor in and director of an MBA program; and Jamie as an experienced leadership consultant and trainer who also had management responsibilities at KPMG, Harbridge House, PricewaterhouseCoopers, Computer Sciences Corporation, and Lexington Leadership Partners.

During our combined 50-plus years of coaching, training, and teaching managers, we have had considerable experience advising an increasing number of people who find themselves in management roles that involve doing as well as leading.

We'll help you succeed as a player-manager by letting go of conventional management thinking and becoming what we call a can-do leader. "Can-do" in the sense that selectively doing hands-on work as a manager becomes an effective strategy for both contributing your professional expertise and for becoming a better leader.

If you are willing to have a go at becoming a can-do leader (CDL), we will show you how to:

- Make the can-do mind shift by being a myth buster (chapter 1).
- Get the right stuff done by thinking TPL (chapter 2).
- Unleash that can-do spirit by checking VITALS (chapter 3).
- Enhance your leadership by selectively engaging in situational doing (chapter 4).
- Build a can-do team by using delegation that emPOWERS (chapter 5).

- Keep improving by creating a can-do learning culture (chapter 6).
- Be a star with career security by becoming a can-do champion (chapter 7).

At the end of each chapter we include a summary called The CDL Playbook to help you master the winning strategies for becoming a can-do leader. A playbook is a sports concept we both learned at an early age; now that we are older, we still find that playbooks help, especially when it comes to mastering leadership skills.

Read on and you'll learn how in the process of becoming a can-do leader you can gain an added influence with your team and in your profession that transforms you from a "too-busy" player-manager into a highly employable leader in your field as a can-do champion.

1

TO MAKE THE CAN-DO MIND SHIFT: BE A MYTH BUSTER

Join us and be a myth buster. A myth buster, that is, with regard to conventional management thinking that holds player-managers back. Consider this for a moment: How many times have people who have become managers heard some version of the following?

- Every time you do work you could have delegated, you're nothing more than the highest paid member of your team.
- If you are not delegating, you are not managing.
- Don't fall into the trap of continuing to do the particular things you really loved doing before you became a manager.
- If you can't let go, you are being controlling and not developing your people.
- If you keep getting caught up in the details of doing work you could have delegated, you'll be "thinking too small to think big."

However, when it comes to the actual practice of being a manager, how many times have many, if not most, managers considered some version of the following?

- The job must get done ASAP, and I am the one person with the expertise to get it done on time.
- I don't trust (or believe) that my people can get the job done on time with the right level of quality.

- I'm concerned that I'm losing my technical relevance because the professional knowledge and skills that I developed prior to becoming a manager are now atrophying.
- Isn't there some way that as a manager I can delegate most tasks, but still get productively involved in other tasks that I might have delegated?

Based on our experience training and coaching player-managers at all levels in a wide range of different situations, the answer to the last question is, most definitely, "Yes, you can." You can both delegate and do as a successful manager. In fact, selectively doing work you might otherwise have delegated enables you to keep up with important technical aspects of your chosen field. Selectively doing can also provide you with opportunities to become a better manager.

We call the misguided belief that if you are not delegating you are not managing the Myth of the Iron Law of Managerial Delegation. Disobeying this hallowed precept of management orthodoxy from time to time does not mean abdicating your managerial responsibility. Even managers who are very skilled at delegating find themselves in situations where this law needs to be bent.

Effective managers understand that focusing on delegating tasks, rather than doing these tasks, is necessary if they are going to get things done and develop their staff along the way. That said, there are times when getting things done properly and developing your staff can be better achieved by doing some tasks yourself rather than delegating all of them.

Some Reasons for Doing Instead of Delegating

Here are some situations where it can be very useful for you, as a manager, to get directly involved in doing work you might have delegated:

- **Leading by example.** Occasionally doing tasks you are still good at highlights your personal commitment to achieving a high performance standard. It also gives you the opportunity to demonstrate strategies and techniques that are useful for excelling at these tasks.

- **Assessing your team members' performance.** Working alongside your colleagues from time to time allows you to assess their on-the-job knowledge and skills so that you have a better idea of their learning gaps and how best to delegate to them in the future.
- **Building team capability.** Being right there with your team gives you opportunities to offer on-the-spot coaching and feedback in areas where you still have special expertise.
- **Improving your team members' morale.** Rolling up your sleeves and helping out when your team is stressed can help lift your team's spirits and increase their respect for you as their leader.
- **Determining if systems and processes are working.** Working alongside your team from time to time gives you the chance to observe firsthand if the way your team is organized is productive, and if your organization's infrastructure and support mechanisms are helping or hindering their ability to perform well.

Of course, you will have to keep in mind that doing work you might have delegated could backfire. When player-managers jump in to do tasks, with little regard for anything other than using their special expertise to get these tasks done properly, time is taken away from managing.

This can also have some unintended side effects that have a negative impact on their ability to lead a team. Team members may get the message that their manager doesn't think they're capable of learning how to do important tasks well, causing them to feel resentment and to become demoralized. They may even conclude that whenever an important task comes along they have to defer to their manager, who will jump in as the "expert" to complete it. This can set in motion an unintended vicious cycle—the more the manager jumps in and does things that the staff might have done, the more the staff becomes dependent upon the manager to do what should be their work. This is not a good way for leaders to manage their time.

Is the problem here the fact that the managers jumped in and did something they might have delegated without considering the potential negative consequences? Perhaps, but not necessarily. More often than not, the real problem is that many, if not most, player-managers get so caught up in a traditional, "either I'm leading or I'm doing" mindset that they fail to see opportunities to address leadership issues while they are doing some of their team's work.

Don't Be Held Back by Either/Or Thinking

The either/or thinking associated with the Myth of the Iron Law of Managerial Delegation encourages people in player-manager roles to adopt the mindset of thinking in terms of, "either I'm leading others or I'm engaged in doing the work myself." Framed this way, time spent doing professional work is time taken away from being a manager. And time spent managing is time taken away from doing professional work.

The zero-sum nature of this either/or mindset leaves player-managers feeling like they are never able to give proper attention to either their leadership role or their continuing professional responsibilities. Instead of feeling that they are growing and filled with a sense of future possibilities, they are more likely to feel frustrated, overwhelmed, and even guilty that they are not measuring up as professionals or as managers.

To take off the either I'm leading or I'm doing mental blinders, start by trying to use the kind of both/and thinking that will enable you to see that many activities associated with being both a professional expert *and* a manager are not necessarily mutually exclusive. Instead, they can be mutually reinforcing.

Too Much on Your Plate? Try Purposeful Multi-Impacting

When you are a leader who is doing some of your team's work, the key is to be mindful of more than the negative impacts you want to avoid. You must also think about how you could help get the task done in a way that also advances your leadership agenda. We call this strategy purposeful *multi-impacting*—getting involved in an activity in a way that offers the promise of achieving more than one objective.

Purposeful multi-impacting describes a more productive way for player-managers to get things done than can be achieved by traditional multi-tasking. Purposeful multi-impacting works because:

- It is often more efficient than multitasking, which usually involves continually switching your attention back and forth between unrelated activities.
- Being aware of the potential positive and negative side effects of actions they might take helps can-do leaders identify good opportunities to advance their leadership agenda while doing tasks.
- Purposeful multi-impacting can be a way for can-do leaders to develop their team members while working alongside them.

Lee, an exceptional engineer, is a nice example of a can-do leader who makes good use of purposeful multi-impacting. Several years ago, he was promoted to the role of manager, but because of economic pressures and his strong engineering credentials, he was also directed to continue doing some of the engineering work. To get the engineering and management results he wanted, Lee decided to be very selective with regard to which engineering work he chose to do. Rather than simply jumping in to take on the tasks he used to like to do, he decided to look for work that gave him the chance to address some of his management responsibilities while also doing engineering tasks.

Following a purposeful multi-impacting leadership strategy, Lee did things like help a recently hired engineer, Joshua, who was behind schedule on an important new product design. Instead of taking over from Joshua to make sure the design was successfully completed, Lee worked alongside Joshua in a purposeful, multi-impacting way. These multi-impacts included:

- **Assessing people while doing.** Lee was able to directly observe Joshua's real, on-the-job skill set, which gave Lee a better idea of how he might make better immediate use of Joshua's skills. Lee also identified a new technical skill that Joshua could develop to be more useful to the team.

- **Sharing expertise with people while doing.** Lee identified opportunities to offer some on-the-job tips that would enable Joshua to complete assignments more effectively and efficiently in the future.
- **Building alignment while doing.** Lee shared war stories with Joshua as they worked together. This gave Joshua a much better idea of the kinds of things their company's marketing people tended to like and dislike in new product designs. Shoptalk not only made Joshua feel more comfortable with Lee, but also reduced the possibility that Joshua would submit new product designs that were likely to be returned for very time-consuming reworks.
- **Assessing the needs of the work environment while doing.** After personally experiencing delays caused by out-of-date software, Lee realized that the expense of replacing the software with an updated package would be more than justified by the increase in his design team's productivity.

Like Lee, if you find yourself saddled with both doing and leading responsibilities, try looking for opportunities to purposefully multi-impact. You might very well find that this will enable you to get more done in less time—and have some fun in the process.

The CDL Playbook

Here's a quick review of the key strategies a can-do leader can use to make the can-do mind shift.

- **Bend the Iron Law of Managerial Delegation.** Be a myth buster and challenge the traditional notion that if you are not delegating, you are not managing. As a myth buster, you will be free to become more successful both as a leader and as a professional.

- **Don't be held back by either/or thinking.** Take off those either/or mental blinders and start using both/and thinking. You'll find that many activities associated with being both a professional expert and a manager can be mutually reinforcing.
- **Get more done by using purposeful multi-impacting.** Whether you are primarily engaged in leading or doing, continue to look for opportunities to talk and act in ways that purposefully achieve more than just one positive outcome.
- **Start enjoying being a can-do leader.** Enjoy taking advantage of the opportunities that come with being a player-manager who has learned how to get things done, and grow professionally as a can-do leader.

What's the next step? Want to be more targeted and successful when using a multi-impacting strategy to fulfill your management responsibilities? In chapter 2, we'll show you how thinking TPL can help you get the right stuff done.

2

TO GET THE RIGHT STUFF DONE: THINK TPL

Chapter 1 introduced the idea of purposeful multi-impacting as a way to get more done in less time. This strategy helps player-managers make decisions and pursue courses of action in ways that simultaneously achieve more than one desired objective.

But when you're in a player-manager position, your goal isn't only to get more done in less time. You also want to make sure that you get the *right* things done as a leader. This means that you need to be purposefully focused on fulfilling your leadership responsibilities, whenever and wherever possible. By the end of this chapter you should have a clear idea of how to do just that.

How can you keep this purposeful focus on *your* leadership agenda? Chances are you've already had a quick look ahead at the answer—the can-do leadership zone (Figure 2-1).

The Can-Do Leadership Zone

This three-dimensional graph represents the fundamental people management responsibilities that *all* leaders inherit when they take on a management position. The three axes—tagged task, people, and learning—are meant to remind us that becoming a player-manager who excels at building teams that get the right things done with high levels of skill and enthusiasm requires giving your continual attention to these three areas.

We call this "thinking TPL" (task, people, learning)—a phrase that could well prove to be a player-manager's best friend.

Figure 2-1. The Can-Do Leadership Zone

Think TPL to Get Into the Can-Do Zone

Thinking TPL can help you remember to do what needs to be done to lead your team into the "can-do zone." This is a place where you and your team can do what needs to be done to meet current and future challenges, and do so with "can-do spirit."

All leaders should start with the task when thinking TPL, because focusing on the work that needs to get done is central to their success. However, they shouldn't lose sight of the fact that eliciting high performance from staff on a sustainable basis requires them to give proper attention to all three dimensions. And, depending on the situation, leaders may need to deliberately emphasize one dimension over another. A team that is new to the work requirements, for example, might need more emphasis on *T*. A team that is frustrated, angry, or anxious might need more emphasis on *P*. A team that is inexperienced might need more emphasis on *L*. Failure to appropriately address these important task, people, and learning issues in a management situation will make it less likely that your players and team will be in the high-performance can-do zone.

How do you think TPL in real time? Kim, a recently promoted manager in an accounting firm, put thinking TPL to good use as she led her first big audit project. Here's how she did it.

Her boss told her that although he wanted her to continue using her considerable auditing expertise to do some pieces of the project, she would ultimately be evaluated not only on how well her team performed, but also on her ability to develop their skills and capabilities. Mindful of the importance of quickly getting her relatively inexperienced team into the can-do zone, Kim used the thinking TPL mantra to help her recognize several opportunities to fulfill her leadership responsibilities.

Thinking *T* reminded Kim that first and foremost her job was to get the audit done correctly and on time. At a minimum, as she led her team through the various phases of the audit, Kim had the continuing responsibility to make sure her team members understood the tasks they needed to perform to achieve the desired results.

Thinking *P*, Kim realized that several of her former peers who now reported to her had been frustrated and unhappy with their past project experiences at this firm. As a result, she needed to find ways to help these team members get fully motivated to drive for high levels of performance.

Thinking *L*, Kim knew she needed to continue to make a conscious effort to find opportunities to develop the current and future capabilities of her team. So when she was considering who would be experienced (T) and motivated (P) to do the work, she also considered giving stretch assignments to develop her people (L) and increase the capabilities and capacity of her team.

When she was doing work alongside her team, Kim worked hard to lead by example and provide clear guidance and direction (T), find ways to engage and motivate her team members (P), and coach and mentor them to accelerate their learning and development (L).

Think TPL So You Aren't Skewed as a Player-Manager

Being "skewed" happens to most of us. In management (and in life), each of us is likely to have particular preferences with regard to dealing with task, people, or learning issues. We call this your "natural first move." Our experience with executive coaching, leadership training, role-play simulations, manager diaries, and the TPL leadership style profiler confirms that whether we realize it or not, we all have distinct preferences. "People persons" like to zero in on the people issues in any situation. Those who are more task oriented like to get right into the details of how to get a particular task done properly. And those who enjoy helping another person or group of people learn how to do something will dive into that aspect of the situation.

Being skewed is fine when you're an individual contributor. Professionals, as individual contributors, often make their mark by being very good along only one dimension. The essence of good management, as Peter Drucker often said, is to put people's strengths to work and to make their limitations irrelevant. A person who is extremely good at addressing task issues but not very good with people can be set to work on nettlesome tasks and buffered from other people. A person who likes to continually learn about new trends and developments can be the go-to person for new ideas, but will not necessarily be the person you rely on to meet tight deadlines.

Being skewed, however, does not work when individual contributors become player-managers. The problem for high-performing professionals who take on a player-manager role is that their typically skewed TPL profile, which wasn't much of a problem when they were individual contributors, can become a big issue when they assume their management role. Their predilection for dealing mostly with task, people, or learning issues means that they typically are not fully cognizant of the broader range of management issues that will need their attention. For example, if they like to focus primarily on task issues, sooner or later the people and learning issues facing their team will become huge problems that dominate their time. Even highly experienced managers, especially when pressured to achieve time-sensitive results, can revert to a skewed, individual contributor mindset when they take on one of their team's tasks.

Managers who focus solely on completing their tasks whenever they are performing hands-on work without considering the potential people and learning issues that might be involved are shirking their leadership responsibilities and are not advancing their leadership agenda. These managers run the risk of significantly limiting the motivation and task capabilities of their team members.

Everyone has a natural tendency when it comes to choosing whether to focus on task, people, or learning issues. And if we don't do something about it, these styles are likely to emerge regardless of the particulars of the management situation we are asked to analyze.

Managers are often surprised to learn their true TPL style. Another interesting finding from our experience is that people often have a different order of preference for dealing with task, people, or learning issues when they feel that things are going well than they do when they are stressed. For example, a person who is very people oriented (high P) when things are going well may become very task oriented (high T) when there is a time crunch. (To learn more about your own TPL style, refer to the Can-Do Leader TPL Leadership Style Profiler in appendix I.)

Take a Power Pause

Becoming aware of your natural TPL tendencies is a good place to start. But it's still too easy, particularly when you are feeling time pressure, to revert to old habits of thinking and yield to your natural first move when you shouldn't. Daniel Kahneman, renowned cognitive psychologist and winner of the Nobel Memorial Prize in Economic Sciences, tells us why this can happen and what to do about it in his very insightful book, *Thinking, Fast and Slow.*

Thinking fast has its uses. Kahneman points out that the fast mode of thinking, widely referred to as System 1 thinking in the field of psychology, can offer many undeniable advantages for functioning successfully as a human being. Being able to suddenly slam on the brakes without giving it conscious thought enables a person to avoid major mishaps when driving a car. In fact much of what we do, be it physical, like using a knife and fork, or mental, like reading a sequence of words, proceeds without much conscious thought.

As Kahneman puts it, System 1 thinking "operates automatically and quickly with little or no effort and no sense of voluntary control." At its most basic level, this kind of thinking enables people to perceive the world around them—recognize objects and orient attention—without having to think about it. System 1's rapid autonomous processes give free reign to impulses and associations. On a higher level, System 1's fast thinking includes mental activities that become rapid and automatic through prolonged practice. Learned associations between ideas will come quickly to mind without any effort. Even highly advanced, intuitive skills—such as a chess master's ability to instantly identify, without conscious thought, possibly useful chess moves—are examples of System 1 fast thinking.

Much has been written of late about the advantages of thinking fast, particularly in the popular press in books such as Malcolm Gladwell's highly entertaining, *Blink: The Power of Thinking Without Thinking*. And, we are indeed lucky that we can think fast in productive ways. But as Kahneman points out, relying solely on System 1 thinking when making important assessments and decisions can often lead people astray.

You can make a big mistake in the blink of an eye! The disadvantages associated with this hyper-fast mode of thinking include reacting only to what we immediately perceive, forming quick impressions without considering further evidence, and rushing to judgment based on heavily biased habits of thought.

Rapid-fire System 1 thinking is useful for effortlessly generating ideas and impressions. But what's also needed, according to Kahneman, is a more deliberate and effortful mode of thinking, known in the field of psychology as System 2 thinking, especially when important assessments and decisions need to be made. This type of thinking helps counter our tendency to jump to conclusions.

But there's a catch here. Yes, it makes sense to slow down our thinking in situations where we are prone to making think-fast mental errors. But it takes a conscious effort to do so. Is pausing to engage in slow, deliberate System 2 thinking worth the effort?

Kahneman reminds us that what at first feels right, may not be right. A counterintuitive finding in his research is that even people who are considered experts in a field can be prone to making poor predictions in their areas of specialty because of their overconfidence in their System-1-generated intuitions. This can happen because of the very human tendency to feel that when ideas come to us quickly and without effort, they are probably good ideas. We tend to place too much confidence in our System-1-generated thoughts and feelings.

It's worth noting that one of the reasons chess masters who can recognize possibly productive moves in an instant are masters is that before actually committing to a move, they typically take the time to think through the potential consequences of their intuitive ideas.

So what does a Nobel Prize winner's research mean for player-managers? If you don't have a routine that becomes a habit for activating System 2 deliberative thinking when you are making important assessments and decisions, you are likely only relying on your think-fast System 1 natural first move. So, even if you know your thinking TPL natural first move, it's useful to have a routine for holding it in check while you deliberately consider other options as well.

We call this "the power pause." Taking a power pause to think TPL gets can-do leaders focused on accomplishing the right things. It's a mental routine that reminds you to look before you leap as a player-manager so you are not dominated by your natural first move when making important management assessments and decisions. Taking a power pause to think TPL will give you the power to slow down your thinking long enough to systematically consider all three dimensions of TPL and identify opportunities to advance your leadership agenda.

Figure 2-2. The Power Pause

Taking power pauses worked for Kim, the player-manager from the accounting firm. According to our TPL leadership style profiler, her natural tendency was to focus on tasks, which had worked fine for her when she was an individual contributor, and no doubt had a lot to do with her promotion. Now, when Kim takes a power pause she takes the time to consider *P* and *L* before taking action.

Making it a habit to take a power pause when facing important management decisions will help keep you focused on fulfilling your leadership responsibilities in a purposeful, systematic way. Having a routine for dealing effectively with your leadership responsibilities will help you feel more confident as you proceed and more in control of your time.

The CDL Playbook

An effective way to use the can-do leadership model is to become aware of your natural first move for addressing task, people, and learning issues.

- **Refer to the Can-Do TPL leadership style profiler** in the appendix to find out what your TPL leadership style is.
- **Take power pauses to think TPL** when addressing important work situations. Start with a clear, objective understanding of the task—the job requirement.
- **Assess the members of your team** to understand what motivates them.
- **Assess what developmental needs can be addressed.**

3

TO UNLEASH THE CAN-DO
SPIRIT: CHECK THEIR VITALS

If you are going to get things done with skill and enthusiasm, you can't simply focus on tasks all the time. It is important instead to take a power pause at critical junctures and think TPL.

This chapter describes a strategy you can use to unleash a level of enthusiasm that embodies the true can-do spirit. Player-managers are well positioned to unleash this spirit in their team members—once they've learned the secret of checking their VITALS.

What Is the Can-Do Spirit?

Someone with the can-do spirit is strongly motivated to demonstrate high levels of commitment, competence, and courage—the 3 Cs—when tackling difficult tasks. Lori, a well-respected national sales manager of a fast-growing industrial products company, is a player-manager who demonstrates these three traits. In addition to managing her team of six regional salespeople, Lori is also responsible for hitting her sales targets for the key national accounts that she personally manages. She was promoted to her position because of her reputation as a high-energy, passionate salesperson, who is driven to excel. When asked to describe how she demonstrates the 3 Cs as a player-manager, Lori said:

- Commitment: "Obsession may be a better word for my desire to exceed my sales targets. Just reaching them never satisfies me."

- Competence: "I never take competence for granted. I always want to keep upping my game. Both as a salesperson, and now as a manager, as well. I want to keep developing my ability to make things happen."
- Courage: "People have called me fearless, but what I really fear is being in my comfort zone too long."

Lori has certainly got the 3 Cs of the can-do spirit, but can she elicit those attributes in others?

If leaders want to see the can-do spirit unleashed in the people who report to them, they've got to feel the 3 Cs themselves. This is particularly true for player-managers who are in frequent contact with their team. You can't expect your team to become committed to an assignment if they sense that their leader doesn't truly believe the assignment is important. Or if they think their leader doesn't believe they have what it takes to get the job done well.

When Lori was promoted, she received a note from her CEO:

> Lori, you're an amazing salesperson—I wish I could clone you. In addition to driving our national accounts as the national sales manager, I also want you to roll up your sleeves, fire up your team, and lead the charge to grow our new Alpha Tech product sales so we are the clear market leader.

When Lori jumped into her new role, she wasn't shy about sharing her enthusiasm with her sales team. Here's an example of a pep talk she gave to her sales team during a weekly conference call:

> We have only three weeks left to beat our end-of-quarter Alpha Tech sales targets. I know you've been hard at it, and some of you are probably feeling pretty exhausted right now. But I also know we can do it.
>
> Sure, we all want those nice bonuses we get for beating our numbers. But this isn't just about money.
>
> I'm out there, just like you, using my relationships with my customers to find ways to close deals as fast as I can.

And I'll bet you are just as excited as I am that we have this great chance now to show how good we are.

And think how great we're going to feel when we prove that no matter how hard the task, we're the kind of people who can make things happen.

Given the responses she heard from her team, Lori was confident her pep talk had inspired them to work even harder to exceed very aggressive end-of-quarter sales targets for the Alpha Tech product line. But Lori went from being pleased to being stunned by what came next. After signing off verbally, she inadvertently stayed on the conference call and proceeded to overhear a conversation between Andy, one of her top performers, and other members of the sales team:

Here we go again. Another "rah-rah" speech from Lori to beat our end-of-quarter sales goals. I know she means well, but just because she's willing to work 24/7 to prove she can meet any challenge, doesn't mean that's what motivates me. I'm thinking about putting my resume out on the street.

The comment was greeted with a few grunts of agreement. Lori's motivational speech had fallen flat. What went wrong?

It is true that sincerely communicating your belief that others can succeed at doing a task can give them extra motivation to succeed. And, the power of negative thinking—projecting your negative belief with words or gestures that a teammate is not up to the task—can be a total turn off. But the power of positive thinking, even when sincerely and eloquently communicated, is unlikely to be enough to unleash the true can-do spirit if it is not supported by another, more vital factor.

So, what is the true source of the can-do spirit?

The VITALS Secret!

People who have the can-do spirit are strongly motivated to demonstrate the 3 Cs—commitment, competence, and courage. And at the center of the 3 Cs is the VITALS core, which is the true source of the can-do spirit

(Figure 3-1). VITALS is an acronym of six key motivational factors: values, interests, talents, ambitions, longings, and style.

Figure 3-1. The Can-Do Spirit

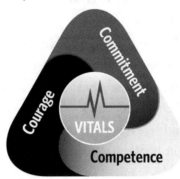

When you can connect the dots between the work people do and their key VITALS motivators, you create the opportunity for their can-do spirit to soar. Here's why each of these six can-do spirit motivators has the power to unleash the energy of your employees:

Values

Values refers to the standards or principles a person believes are important to uphold in life, which could include things like trustworthiness, service to others, loyalty, fairness, cultural dictates, and other deeply held beliefs.

A person's values are important to consider when giving an assignment because if you ask someone to behave in a way that goes against what he believes in, you may end up motivating him to work against you. In a diverse workplace it is particularly important for leaders to appreciate the power of the cultural beliefs of their teams. For example, if Peter comes from a culture where being singled out for public praise is embarrassing, he will likely be more appreciative and energized if you praise him in private.

Interests

Interests are the work-related subject areas that grab and hold a person's attention. The deeper a person's interest in something, the stronger her motivation will be to work on projects that allow her to pursue that interest. The curiosity associated with strong interests is what motivates the kind of learning that pays dividends in the workplace. For example, if John loves to solve problems, giving him an opportunity to solve a complex customer fulfillment issue is likely to pique his interests in a way that truly unleashes his can-do spirit.

Talents

Talents refer not only to skills that a person may have developed, but also to the underlying ability or aptitude that makes it possible for him to develop a noteworthy skill.

When people have a strong talent in a particular area, they often enjoy developing and displaying that talent. The key is to identify those talents. For example, if Maria is very skilled at creating innovative software designs and likes to talk about her creations, giving her opportunities to use this talent on the job is likely to be very motivating for her.

Ambitions

Ambitions are the goals a person has for both his career and his personal life—what he wants to be and achieve.

Giving people assignments, when you can, that make them feel like they are pursuing important career goals can be a strong motivator. For example, if Adam has aspirations for management roles, giving him an opportunity to manage an engineering project is likely to be highly motivating for him.

Longings

Longings are the nagging (when not sufficiently satisfied) psychological needs people bring to the workplace. Psychologist David McClelland, known for his research on motivation, proposed a Need Theory, which describes the human need for achievement, affiliation, power, and autonomy. These needs are often found in the workplace, along with the need for adventure and creativity, and a desire for stability and predictability.

For example, if Trish has strong relationship needs, she is likely to be most engaged when given opportunities to work in a group. Conversely, if

Damita has a low need for affiliation, but a very high need for autonomy, she is likely to be more motivated when given opportunities to work independently.

Style

Style at work refers to a person's characteristic ways of taking in information, making decisions, dealing with success and failure, and interacting with others. The style concept focuses on preferences rather than abilities. When we understand other people's personal style, we are better able to find effective ways of being influential with them.

For example, if Pablo is a planner and likes to be well organized and structured in how he approaches work, giving him an assignment that allows him to draw on this preferred style is likely to increase his level of motivation.

The can-do spirit is most likely to be released in people when their most important VITALS can be satisfied at work. And when you start to find ways to connect your team members' key VITALS to the work you want them to do, they will start to have a stronger sense of ownership (commitment). You will also see them taking more initiative to apply and develop their expertise (competence). And you will see them becoming more confident as they embrace stretch assignments (courage). In short, you will start to see the 3 Cs of the true can-do spirit.

How About Your VITALS?

We have an easy way for you to remember what it feels like when you have that can-do spirit. It's called the can-do spirit VITALS checkup. And it's waiting for you in appendix II.

The VITALS checkup provides a simple strategy you can use to identify the kinds of tasks and projects that are most likely to unleash your can-do spirit at work.

Once you understand your own motivational triggers, you will be better able to look at what motivates the people who report to you in a way that is not biased by your personal preferences.

How Well Do You Know Your Team's VITALS?

Leaders are often asked how well they know their people. More often than not the reply is "quite well" or words to that effect. But when some specific questions are posed about how well they know such things as their team members' values, interests, and ambitions, it is not unusual to get an embarrassed look.

Use Your CDL Advantage

You may be thinking, "The check their VITALS strategy sounds like a good idea for understanding what motivates others, but how can I possibly find out all these things about the people who work with me?"

If you are a player-manager, being positioned as both a leader and a doer can be a big help. A general rule for checking someone's VITALS is to ask, listen, and observe. And player-managers can often do this in much greater depth than traditional managers because they are doers as well as leaders. Here are a few ways you can use the CDL advantage to help check their VITALS:

- The first step, of course, is to understand your VITALS. You can't truly understand other people's VITALS if you don't understand how your own motivational profile influences your thinking and feeling.
- Use both your leader and your doer roles to check your team members' VITALS. As a player-manager, you have many opportunities to ask questions and observe your team members in action. If you are mindful of the importance of checking their VITALS, you can use these occasions to get a better understanding of their key motivators.
- Use the VITALS acronym as a checklist to help you come up with good questions. Ask about the kinds of activities and assignments they find most interesting, as well as their near- and long-term career ambitions and what they think might be their strongest talents. Listen carefully to their responses.
- Observe possible VITALS indicators. For example, when working alongside your team members, observe their reactions

to different situations and assignments. Reflecting on these observations can help you better understand important aspects of your team members' VITALS motivational profiles.

- Do not put yourself in the other person's shoes. This is misleading advice. Demonstrating empathy is often well meant, but because people have their own set of personal motivators, we can't simply project our own motivational profile onto another person. What would motivate you in a situation is irrelevant to someone else. Real empathy occurs when you begin to understand what truly motivates others—from their point of view.

- Take VITALS power pauses to avoid narrow framing. Just as everyone has a natural first move with regard to TPL, we're also likely to have a strong preference when it comes to the VITALS factors we believe are most important. If we are not careful, our personal preferences will bias our assessment of other people's VITALS profiles.

As we discussed in the last chapter, Daniel Kahneman (2011) has found that if we do not have routines for activating deliberative thinking, we are very likely to use narrow framing when assessing what we perceive to be familiar situations. Instead of methodically considering a sufficiently wide range of possibilities that might explain what's happening (broad framing), we are very likely to quickly zero in on the things we are accustomed to associating with the situation we are dealing with.

Kahneman points out that until the early 1950s doctors and other health professionals relied on their "intuitive" gut reaction to determine whether a newborn needed immediate medical attention to survive. As a result, these professionals would often focus very narrowly on the one or two things they thought were necessary to assess to decide if the baby was OK. However, in 1953, Dr. Virginia Apgar introduced the broad-framing APGAR checklist (appearance, pulse, grimace, activity, and respiration) to help physicians make a systematic assessment of whether immediate medical intervention was necessary. This new routine effectively created a power pause moment that has saved countless lives.

While taking a power pause to check their VITALS may not save your team members' lives, it may very well help you unleash a highly sustainable can-do spirit. You'll never learn everything there is to know about another person's motivators. But if you ask, listen, and observe, you'll know a lot more about what motivates your team members than you did before. And when you give them an assignment, you'll be better able to release their can-do spirit.

How Would This Look in the Real World?

Let's circle back to Lori. You can imagine the frustration and disappointment she must have felt when she realized that her regional sales representatives weren't as energized by the prospect of meeting a difficult challenge as she was.

We started working with Lori after her team failed to hit their third-quarter Alpha Tech sales targets. We saw pretty quickly that Lori was, in effect, projecting her own motivational profile onto her team members—assuming that they, being salespeople, would be motivated by the same things that motivated her.

After Lori took the can-do spirit VITALS checkup, she identified her top three can-do motivators, which she put in the following order of importance:

1. Longings: "Guess I'm what you might call a challenge junkie. My number one motivator for sure is proving that I can meet the really tough, impossible challenges. Just knowing I've got some tough sales targets to beat really gets me jazzed."

2. Style: "I really enjoy building relationships with people in ways that can be mutually beneficial. This probably explains why I connect so well with my customers."

3. Interests: "I love being in situations where I need to keep learning new things. I love keeping up-to-date in my field. I'm always trying to learn whatever I can about what's new in our industry, what's happening with our customers and our competitors, and how it will affect us."

Lori had no trouble understanding that her self-described top motivator—her passion for achieving seemingly impossible goals—was what had driven her to become Salesperson of the Year for two years in a row. But the challenge of stepping up to beat aggressive sales targets wasn't necessarily the primary source of motivation for her sales reps, as was obvious from the conversation she overheard after her failed pep talk.

Then we asked her, "Do you ever treat your sales team like customers?" That made her think.

It turned out that like many excellent salespeople who are promoted to manager, Lori wasn't interacting with her new direct reports with the style that she used with customers (finding out what turned them on by asking lots of questions). Instead she was thinking of her new player-manager role as one in which she had to present herself as the Be-Like-Lori role model her boss had told her he wanted to clone.

Referring to her VITALS profile, we reminded Lori that she seemed to thoroughly enjoy using an interpersonal style that created mutually beneficial relationships with her customers. And she had a strong interest in learning about the evolving needs and wants of her customers. These were two key motivators that no doubt contributed to her ability to get customers excited about the products she was selling.

Would the interpersonal style that Lori used to develop mutually beneficial relationships with her customers also work with her team? Lori was encouraged to take advantage of the opportunities she had to work alongside her sales representatives to get to know their wants and needs, just as she liked to do with her customers.

Thereafter, whenever Lori traveled with members of her sales team, she made a conscious effort to ask questions that would give her a better sense of the kind of opportunities, coaching, and encouragement that would be most motivating for each member of her team.

Example 1

Lori did not tell Andy she had overheard his complaint after her failed pep talk. But here's how she handled her next sales trip with him, ostensibly to assist him while he presented their line of products to several of his key accounts. She knew that he was good at meeting his sales targets and she didn't want him to put his resume out on the street, particularly because he was greatly respected by the other salespeople on her team.

What struck Lori while they visited his accounts was that Andy didn't need any help from her when presenting the product line. He could handle highly technical questions quite convincingly on his own. But what impressed her most was the change that came over Andy when he introduced the two new products that had been added to the line several days before. He had an almost mesmerizing talent for explaining the features and benefits of these technically sophisticated products, including many details and benefits that weren't even mentioned in the product literature. And he was doing this for two products that he had only seen for the first time a few days ago.

That evening at dinner Lori told Andy how impressed she was: "I must say, I'm feeling a little envious. Right out of the box you have an unusually good sense of how these products can be put to good use. What's the trick? How do you learn so much about these products so quickly?"

In the conversation that followed Lori learned that unlike her other sales representatives, Andy had a degree in engineering and had worked as an engineer for several years before going into sales. "I still have an engineer's love of learning about new technical things," he explained. "So it's a lot of fun for me to think about how our new products can be put to best use."

When she asked Andy why he had switched over to sales, he paused and then said, "Frankly, Lori, because when I was an engineer, I couldn't stand having a boss ride herd on me. That's just not my style. Don't take this personally, but I like to think I'm pretty much my own boss when I am in sales. So long as I meet my boss's expectations . . . provided they're reasonable, that is."

"Would it be a 'reasonable expectation' if I asked you to make more use of your extraordinary interests and talents in the technical area?" Lori asked.

This question piqued Andy's curiosity. Lori proposed that "as partners" several times a year, Andy help her present new products to some of her most promising national account sales leads.

This turned the lights on for Andy. His passion for describing how the technology in their new products could yield great benefits for potential clients helped Lori close on several key national accounts several months later.

And they really did become more like partners than manager and direct report. Whenever a new product was introduced, Lori asked Andy to share his thoughts on the best way to present the technical features and benefits with other members of the sales force during their conference calls and during national sales meetings. She also made sure that Andy had direct contact with a lead engineer at the company so he could pass along any ideas for technical innovations in new products.

Energized by the opportunities and thoughtful attention Lori had given him, Andy made sure he continued to hit his sales targets.

Not only did Andy not put his resume out on the street; he also became one of Lori's most trusted and enthusiastic supporters.

Example 2

Lori knew that Melissa was a real people person who had always been wonderful at building and maintaining friendly and helpful relationships with her accounts. So Lori was surprised when during a shared road trip, she noticed that Melissa wasn't showing her usual enthusiasm. Behind Melissa's forced smiles, Lori could sense that her spirits were down. Asking Melissa how things were going in general, she learned that Melissa's youngest child had recently left for college and had been increasingly distancing herself from her mother. "She's really gone. And not just physically," is the way Melissa summed it up.

While sympathizing with Melissa, Lori had a great VITALS-inspired idea. She had recently traveled with Andrea, a new hire in her early twenties who was very enthusiastic about her job and had a great people-oriented sales personality. But she was also full of rookie questions and wanted help from an older, more experienced salesperson who knew how to get things done the right way.

Lori loved Andrea's enthusiasm, but she was too busy with her own responsibilities to give Andrea the kind of attention she needed. But what about Melissa? She had a talent for developing accounts, a helpful style, and now a youngest-daughter-sized hole in her heart.

"It was like throwing a switch," Lori said, remembering the burst of excitement when she asked Melissa if she would be willing to spend a week traveling with Andrea. Lori also suggested Melissa mentor Andrea if the trip went well.

No surprise, Melissa and Andrea became fast friends. They continued to talk and text about how things were going long after their business trip was over. Andrea's sales numbers were soon quite extraordinary for someone in her first sales job. And, despite the extra time Melissa had been devoting to helping Andrea, her sales numbers went up significantly too.

When Lori thanked Melissa for continuing to help Andrea and also congratulated her on her strong sales numbers at the end of the year, Melissa explained, "The thanks should be coming from me, really. Becoming friends with Andrea was just what this empty-nester needed. It really reminded me how important continuing to be helpful is to me. More than one of my old accounts has asked me, 'What's going on? You've got so much energy these days!'"

What if Work Requirements Are a VITALS Mismatch?

What if there's something important that needs to get done and there's no one available on your team whose VITALS motivators match up with the task? Here's our best advice:

Honesty is still the best policy. Let the person who gets a VITALS mismatch assignment know that you realize this is not going to be one of his favorite assignments, and explain why you're in this situation. Tell him you know you can depend on him to give it his best shot. And he's likely to do just that—especially if you've given him many assignments that he has found highly motivating in the past.

But this strategy is only possible if you have already made the effort to find out what truly motivates your teammates. And for this we once again suggest that you check their VITALS.

The CDL Playbook

To unleash the can-do spirit in yourself and others, be sure to make good use of the following strategies:

- **Don't forget that the true source of a person's can-do spirit is her VITALS.**
- **Know your VITALS:**
  - to discover the true source of your can-do spirit
  - to understand your natural first move.
- **Use your CDL advantage:**
  - to regularly check up on the VITALS of your teammates by using your positioning as both leader and doer
  - to check someone's VITALS by remembering to ask, listen, and observe.
- **Take VITALS power pauses:**
  - to avoid being dominated by your own VITALS profile when assessing others
  - to avoid narrow framing.
- **Be mindful of VITALS when you assign work:**
  - to unleash your team members' can-do spirit
  - to know when you are giving an assignment that is a VITALS mismatch.

4

TO ENHANCE YOUR LEADERSHIP: ENGAGE IN SITUATIONAL DOING

Good leadership is situational in the sense that the best leadership strategy to use typically depends on the situation the leader is facing. We've coined the term *situational doing* to underscore the fact that to be effective as a player-manager, you need to be very selective with regard to *when* and *how* you do work that you might have delegated.

This chapter discusses how the thought processes you developed in chapters 2 and 3 can help you decide when to delegate and when to do the work yourself. Thinking TPL and conducting VITALS checkups can help you engage in situational doing in ways that advance your leadership agenda, maintain your professional competence, and improve your overall business impact.

What You Think Is "Mine" Can Be a Minefield

Situational doing can only be effective if it is done in a highly selective and informed way by managers. For example, Charlie is a top performer at an aerospace company. He is a gifted engineer who has taken on significant responsibilities as the manager of the fast-growing flight controls software design department, as well as the lead software design engineer of a major aerospace flight controls project.

Charlie rose to his player-manager responsibilities largely because of his stellar reputation for software engineering design. He is considered to be one of the company's leading engineers, which led to his current promotion. However, as the company has grown, the productivity of his department has fallen—in part because Charlie insists on doing many of the most complex tasks on his own.

Charlie defends doing much of his team's work himself, saying: "Look, I still enjoy doing the advanced technical stuff—and frankly, I'm good at it. I'm often not very confident that my people can do it right. I know I should probably spend more time developing them, but I don't have much time to train them. Bottom line, when I do it myself, I know I'll get the job done right."

Have you ever found yourself in that vicious cycle where you keep doing work that you should delegate? Charlie means well, but his "what's mine is mine" mindset regarding his team's work means that his team is not developing at a pace that is keeping up with the needs of the company. He knows he is doing work that he should have delegated, but he doesn't have a mental routine for deciding when to do and when to delegate.

When this happens, Charlie misses out on opportunities to develop his team members' capabilities to do the work that needs to be done today and in the future. Imagine how his team members feel when they see their boss doing work that they could or should be doing themselves. What signals do they pick up about the trust their boss has in them, and the level of interest he has in helping them develop?

Thinking like a can-do leader can help Charlie become more system-atically thoughtful about what tasks to do and what work to delegate. By doing so he increases the odds that whether doing or delegating, his actions are consciously designed to further his leadership agenda.

The first rule to follow for achieving the proper balance with regard to doing and delegating is to avoid falling into the trap of mindlessly assign-ing yourself whatever work you most enjoy doing. We have a strategy for avoiding the pitfall of mindlessly thinking that "it's mine!"

To Be Mindful of Your Personal Minefield—Check Your VITALS

It is important that you understand which of your personal motivators could inappropriately dominate your thinking when it's time for you to decide who should be doing a particular task. (The can-do spirit VITALS checkup in appendix II can help you identify your dominant motivators.)

Once you know your dominant motivators, taking a VITALS power pause to make sure you are not being unduly swayed by these motivators can help you avoid the perils of self-only thinking. Being a player-manager does not give you permission do a particular task simply because you wanted to do it yourself.

The Good, the Not So Good, and the Ugly

The burden falls on leaders to put the needs of their teams first when deciding when to get involved in work they might have delegated. That said, there are a number of reasons to get involved. This choice must take into consideration the VITALS of the team as well as your own VITALS. You need to be aware of not only the good reasons for jumping in, but also the potentially bad reasons for doing so.

The Good

Doing work yourself for the right reasons can be good. If you do professional work in ways that develop the capabilities and confidence of your team, doing becomes a strategy you can use from time to time to further your leadership agenda. Here are some examples of doing professional work in ways that reinforce your leadership role:

Leading by example—Sometimes it is appropriate to set an example of the high performance standards you expect of yourself and others by doing a task in a way that demonstrates how you apply your professional knowledge, expertise, and judgment.

Demonstrating your personal commitment to your team members—When you work alongside others, you can interact with them, listen to their needs and concerns, and show interest in their success.

Observing possible VITALS indicators—When you work alongside your team members, you can directly observe their reactions to different situations and assignments. Reflecting on these observations can help you better understand your team members' key VITALS motivators.

Assessing your team members' actual performance—When you want to check how effectively your colleagues are performing, working alongside them allows you to assess their on-the-job strengths and weaknesses. This can give you a better idea of what their learning needs are and how best to deploy them now and in the future.

Building team capability through on-the-fly training and coaching— Working alongside your team gives you the ability to offer real-time coaching and feedback in areas where you have special expertise. You'll learn more about this in chapter 6.

Inspiring your team members when they are facing a tough challenge—Being willing to jump into the fray to help your team when they are stressed can lift their spirits and morale and increase their respect for you as their leader

Assessing the effectiveness of systems and processes effective—Helping your team from time to time allows you to observe if your team is organized in a way that is productive and if your organization's infrastructure and support mechanisms are helping or hindering their functioning.

Staying current in the technical aspects of your field—As the leader of your team, you certainly can't be an expert in all the technical areas that report to you. But periodically doing some professional work yourself can help you stay sufficiently technically informed so you can continue having productive conversations with the knowledge workers who report to you.

When, as a player-manager, you have to make sure you're doing something for the right reasons, you can no longer approach doing as an individual contributor. Instead, you must deliberately find ways to build the capabilities and confidence of your team.

The Not So Good

Sometimes you have to do professional work yourself simply because there's no reasonable alternative. Have you found yourself in one of the following situations?

Got to get it done under severe time pressure—Having all hands on deck, including yours, may be the only way you can avoid the consequences of missing a drop-dead deadline. But the fact that you had to step in and do some of the work yourself may suggest either poor planning or a failure to develop the capabilities of your staff.

Need to plug holes because you are continually short-handed—If you simply do not have enough people to do all the work you are responsible for managing, you will likely have to do some of it yourself more often than you want. This may indicate a failure to manage your staffing in a way that maintains the appropriate number of people with the requisite capabilities.

Some team members are not performing at the required standard—Finding yourself having to redo important assignments that team members have messed up may be the only way that these tasks get done properly in the required timeframe. However, this may indicate that you have not been providing sufficient guidance and direction for them. You may need to pay more attention to developing their skills or you may not be facing up to a necessary termination decision.

If you find yourself doing a lot of work for expedient reasons, it could be a signal that you need to refocus your delegation and doing decisions in ways that better develop your team members.

The Ugly

Doing for inappropriate reasons is the ugly. Here are some classic reasons why managers fail to delegate a task. Are you guilty of any of these?

Can't let go because you like the feeling of being in control—If you don't let your staff do the majority of their tasks because you fear losing control, you'll end up losing control of your ability to function as an effective manager.

Lack of confidence in your own skill as a delegator—The less you delegate, the less confidence you'll have in your ability to delegate assignments effectively. There's an easy fix here: Read chapter 5 to learn how to delegate in a way that "emPOWERS" success.

Impatience—Believing that time is being wasted whenever things are not done as quickly as you think you could do them can cause you to do tasks you should have delegated.

Belief that others can't do a particular task as well as you—You may be right that no one else can do a job as well as you. But here's the real question: Is there someone else who can do the job well enough? Perhaps with a little coaching?

Ignoring the VITALS of others—Not considering your team members' VITALS motivators may make it easier to justify doing the work yourself, but it also limits their development opportunities. It can also put a damper on their spirits.

Doing professional work for inappropriate reasons sends a sour message to your team—They may believe you have a negative view of their abilities and a lack of interest in helping them develop and succeed. The fact that you are not placing a priority on ensuring your team members learn and grow means that your staff is likely to be progressively less able to do the work you should be delegating to them.

To Do the Right Things, "Get Situational"

Before you can make an effective decision as to whether you should do a task you might have delegated, you first need to have a good understanding of the particular situation you find yourself in.

Thinking TPL as you review the salient features of the situation can help you identify the key task, people, and learning issues you should be considering as a player-manager.

The can-do leadership illustration provides some reminders of the kinds of things that would be helpful to know about your situation (Figure 4-1).

Periodically reviewing this graphic can help you develop the habit of thinking TPL as you go about carrying out your duties as a player-manager. This will help you quickly identify and access the kind of knowledge you need when you are wrestling with do-or-delegate decisions.

Figure 4-1. Can-Do Leadership Overview

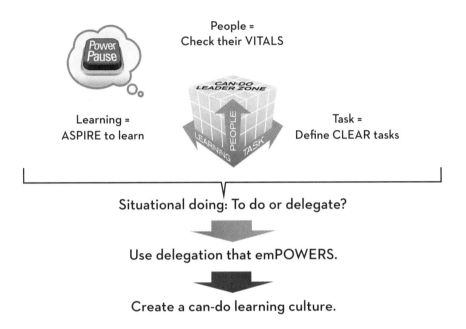

Consider: The Situational Doing Protocol

To help organize your thinking, use the situational doing protocol (sit-do protocol, for short) to understand how to access your TPL and VITALS knowledge to determine when doing tasks you might have delegated is good, not so good, or even downright ugly.

The decision tree graphic doesn't represent ironclad rules; instead, it is a way of presenting the key things to consider as you think through a do-or-delegate decision (Figure 4-2).

Thinking TPL on Two Levels

When deciding whether to do or to delegate, it is helpful to be able to Think TPL on two levels.

Figure 4-2. Decision Tree Graphic

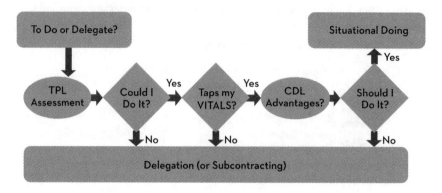

The Team Level

Thinking TPL on the team level means being able to assess the key task, people, and learning issues that are likely to affect your team's overall ability to address current and future needs. Ask yourself these questions when thinking TPL on the team level:

- T = What sort of work does my team need to be able to excel at today? In the future? To what extent does my team understand our overall business situation, our customer requirements, and our most important priorities?
- P = Do we have people who are able to excel at the work we need to do right now? Will enough people be ready for the future? How motivated is my team to do the work we must do? Is there an overall sense of the can-do spirit?
- L = What further knowledge and skills does my team need to acquire to be ready for the challenges we face today and in the future?

The Individual Performance Level

Thinking TPL on the individual performance level means being able to assess the key task, people, and learning issues that are likely to affect the readiness of each team member to perform the work you want them to do now and in the future. Ask yourself these questions when thinking TPL on the individual level:

- T = Will the person to whom I am considering giving this task easily understand the requirements? If not, how much time now, and possibly during the assignment, will I have to spend making sure he understands what he is meant to do?
- P = Does this person have the necessary knowledge and skills to do this task at the required speed and level of performance? What about her level of motivation, given her VITALS profile?
- L = Are there significant learning gaps? If so, how much help and time would he need to learn the necessary skills? Would developing him along these lines make him a more useful player on your team?

Being able to answer these questions on both levels will give you a good starting point when deciding whether to do or to delegate.

Let Charlie Show You

Following the sit-do protocol is not nearly as complicated as it may seem. For example, consider how Charlie, the software design engineer turned player-manager, used the protocol.

Because of his deep expertise in flight controls software design, Charlie rose quickly through the ranks of his aerospace company. However, he became an unhappy player-manager, and was increasingly frustrated that his team members weren't able to get things done at his accustomed speed and level of quality. As a result, he felt like he had to continually jump in and do things himself. But as he began doing more and more, he realized that his strategy of "if you want it done right, do it yourself" wasn't working for him or for his disgruntled team, whose productivity was falling. Now that he was responsible for his team's overall performance, Charlie realized that he needed to re-engineer how he was doing his player-manager job.

The TPL leadership style profiler showed that Charlie's natural first move was to focus on task, with learning coming a close second. He also completed the can-do spirit VITALS checkup exercise to understand his key motivators. That done, Charlie considered how to use the sit-do protocol.

What did thinking TPL at the team and individual performance levels tell Charlie? He identified his team's current strengths and weaknesses for the key tasks that needed to be done, the people who might be able to do these tasks, and the learning gaps that existed. Thinking TPL at the team level forced Charlie to face up to the fact that his team was not developing in ways that would allow them to keep up with client demand. And they weren't nearly as excited about getting stuff done as he was. Thinking TPL at the individual performance level helped Charlie discover that he didn't know his people very well. He saw that the one-size-fits-all approach to improving each individual's level of performance he had been using would not work for his team.

As a player-manager, Charlie had many opportunities when he was delegating and doing to get to know his team members' VITALS profiles. He realized that continuing to take power pauses to think TPL and check VITALS would help him understand his people and allow him to make more informed do-or-delegate decisions.

Questions to Think About

Could Charlie do some of the work his team needs to do? Yes, there are many situations where he has the skills to do work he might have assigned, but according to the sit-do protocol, that doesn't mean Charlie should automatically do the work.

What sort of professional work really taps Charlie's vitals motivators? Taking the VITALS checkup reminded Charlie that:

- His software design interests and talents and his desire for challenging mental stimulation motivated him to take on complex design work whenever he could.
- His personal style was to do as much of this analytical work as he could on his own.
- He valued the "spirit of inquiry" and it was a personal ambition to be part of a continuous learning culture wherever he worked.

What are the key CDL advantages in play here? To help Charlie better understand this question, he needs to let go of the individual contributor mindset that he has when doing professional work. Instead, he needs to start adopting the mindset of a can-do leader who is ever mindful of the leadership opportunities associated with doing. Charlie reviewed the doing for the right reasons and doing for inappropriate reasons lists to better understand the differences between a can-do leader's approach and individual contributor thinking. It was clear from Charlie's initial team-level TPL assessment that his team was dispirited and not developing in productive ways. To address these issues, Charlie needed to get a better understanding of his individual team member's VITALS profiles.

Should Charlie do the work? Clearly he can do many tasks himself rather than delegate. And his VITALS profile underscored the fact that his talents, interests, and longings all motivated him to take on complex design work whenever he could. However, thinking TPL at the team level forced him to recognize that his team was not nearly as motivated as he was to get things done. And his team members also didn't seem to be developing in ways that would enable them to keep up with future demands. As Charlie took another look at the doing for the right reasons list, he decided he should give top priority when he was engaged in doing professional work to:

- Demonstrate personal commitment to the team members.
- Observe possible vitals indicators.
- Assess team members' actual performance.
- Build team capability through on-the-spot coaching.

But Charlie was still hesitant to fully embrace this approach to situational doing, which brought him back to a discussion of his VITALS profile. The VITALS motivator holding him back was his do-it-alone style—his preference for doing as much of the design work as he could on his own, not with others. If he was going to achieve the leadership priorities he had identified, Charlie needed to put more emphasis on working with others when doing the design work he loved to do.

Charlie's VITALS profile left no doubt that he valued the spirit of inquiry and that it was a personal ambition of his to be part of a continuous learning culture wherever he worked. So he decided to use a style of situational doing that included facilitating learning to give him the opportunity to champion a work culture that put a greater emphasis on the spirit of inquiry.

Did everything work out fine for Charlie and his team from that moment on? No, he still had a few bumps in the road; becoming an effective can-do leader is a process, not a quick fix. But the sit-do protocol showed Charlie a way to start making sensible do-or-delegate decisions. It enabled him to let go of his "if you want it done right, do it yourself" strategy, and start focusing on doing professional work in ways that developed his team's competence and confidence.

As Charlie got to know his team better using the sit-do protocol, he was able to delegate much of the work he had previously thought that he needed to do himself. When he chose to do professional work himself, he was more likely to do so with a leadership purpose in mind. And this resulted in more productivity, a better can-do spirit, and more time for Charlie to focus on the things that were important for him to focus on in his leadership position.

Think TPL While Engaged in Situational Doing

Making a conscious effort to think TPL while doing professional work that might have been delegated will prevent you from reverting back to the narrow mindset of an individual contributor. Here are some examples of how thinking TPL can help you become a can-do leader who is making effective use of situational doing.

Thinking Task While Doing

Rather than getting filtered, secondhand reports of what's happening when your team members are at work, you can see for yourself and give them whatever they need to get tasks done right. However, be mindful of the dangers of micromanaging, and ask questions in a supportive way (Table 4-1).

Thinking People While Doing

Working alongside your team members will give you opportunities traditional managers rarely, if ever, get to directly assess motivational and interpersonal issues that surface while your team members are carrying out their assignments.

How you behave when you are working alongside your team members will have a lot to do with how they behave in your presence. If you are supportive, over time your team members will be more likely to be themselves in their interactions with you and other teammates (Table 4-2).

Table 4-1: Examples of Thinking Task While Doing

Examples of What You Want	How Situational Doing Helps
Are your delegated instructions clearly understood?	In addition to leading by example, you can clarify how the work your team is doing supports their mission.
Is the work being carried out in ways that are likely to meet client expectations?	If relevant, explain what adjustments need to be made to meet the expectations of your internal or external customers.
Is the work being organized, staffed, and supported in ways that promote success?	Experiencing firsthand the challenges your team is facing puts you in a good position to identify necessary changes.
Will the work be done on time?	Observe any bottlenecks, issues, or challenges to doing things in a timely fashion and remove them.

Table 4-2: Examples of Thinking People While Doing

Examples of What You Want	How Situational Doing Helps
Is your team highly motivated to do the work?	Working alongside your team members can give you the opportunity to sense your team's mood when engaged in different kinds of projects.
What information will inform your future delegation of assignments?	Directly observing your team at work will help you think of questions you can ask to gain a better understanding of your team members' VITALS profiles.
What will unleash the can-do spirit in your team members?	This VITALS information can help to improve your delegation of assignments.
How can you improve team dynamics?	Experiencing your team members' current level of communications, their willingness to support one another, and their ability to provide constructive feedback can suggest things you might do to improve team dynamics.

Thinking Learning While Doing

Doing as a can-do leader gives you the opportunity to identify individual and organizational learning gaps. You can create targeted development plans to increase the capabilities of your team (Table 4-3).

Table 4-3. Examples of Thinking Learning While Doing

Examples of What You Want	How Situational Doing Helps
Do you have an accurate assessment of the knowledge, skills, and experience of your team?	Working alongside team members gives you a firsthand look at their current strengths and development needs.
How can you accelerate your team members' abilities to get the knowledge and skills they need to better meet current and future demands?	While doing, you will be able to not only coach team members, but also discuss other ways that they can learn the things they need to learn now and in the future.
Are you current in your personal area of professional expertise?	Selectively choosing certain types of assignments can help you maintain the level of technical competence you need to stay relevant in your professional area of expertise.

Warning: The LENS Will Be Tightly Focused on You

Whenever you engage in situational doing as a player-manager your team members will attend to the smallest details of what you say and do, especially your tone of voice, gestures, and facial expressions. Even your off-the-cuff wisecracks that aren't meant to be taken seriously will be scrutinized and circulated far more than when you were just another team member. Members of a team tend to view formally appointed leaders through a lens—the word *lens* can be thought of as an acronym for leadership effect never stops.

Can-do leaders can take advantage of the magnifying power of the lens. When you work alongside those who report to you, don't act like a know-it-all micromanager who is frustrated by the team's limitations. Instead, be an effective can-do leader by motivating your team members through your belief that they have what it takes to get better and better.

The CDL Playbook

The following mental reframes associated with the can-do mind shift will help you recognize and take advantage of the many leadership opportunities associated with situational doing for the right reasons:

- **From doing for self-centered reasons to getting situational:** Using the sit-do protocol will help you be mindful of what you need to know to make well-informed do-or-delegate decisions.

- **From thinking as an individual contributor to thinking TPL:** When doing professional work, never lose sight of the fact that you're not an individual contributor anymore. Making a conscious effort to think TPL will prevent you from reverting to the narrow mindset of an individual contributor.

- **From multitasking to multi-impacting:** Focus on multi-impacting to make sure the work you choose to do allows you to get professional work done, but also advances your leadership agenda. Thinking both/and rather than either/or will enable you to make the best use of your time as a player-manager.

- **From seeing either the management big picture or the worker's details to being able to see both:** As you learn more about what's actually happening when your team members are working, you can test the validity of your current big picture management strategies against the realities that your teammates are facing.

- **From thinking you are still one of the gang to taking advantage of the LENS:** Remember that when you jump in and do work alongside your team members, you may feel like you're one of the gang again. But that's definitely *not* how your team members will see you: The leadership effect never stops. If you can't get it working for you, it's probably working against you.

5

TO BUILD A CAN-DO TEAM: USE DELEGATION THAT emPOWERS

While it is true that in this book we introduce a new leadership strategy called situational doing, which encourages managers to selectively do work they might have delegated, we are not recommending that *doing* should take priority over *delegating* as a way for can-do leaders to get things done. We are proposing that, contrary to popular wisdom, doing some of the work you might have delegated can actually help you become better at delegating—better, that is, at employing the kind of delegation that fully empowers teams to succeed. At the end of the day, this results in getting things done faster, better, and cheaper.

Unleashing a strong can-do spirit is not all that's needed to bring about peak performance. Can-do leaders also need to bring to life a form of empowerment when delegating assignments that is fully informed by their situational doing. We call this "emPOWERSment."

Why emPOWERSment?

Well, the word definitely gets your attention. More important, there are six qualities associated with a person becoming fully empowered to successfully carry out an assignment. The word *powers* can be used as an acronym to help you remember what these qualities are:

- **Proficiency** is the extent to which a person has the basic knowledge, experience, and skills to do a particular assignment properly.
- **Obligation** refers to the particulars of the assignment that is being delegated. What exactly is the person who has been given the assignment obligated to do?
- **Willingness** is a direct report's level of motivation to do a particular assignment beyond obligatory compliance.
- **Encouragement** can help a person feel confident when confronting a daunting task.
- **Resources** necessary for successfully carrying out an assignment must be allocated when and where they are needed.
- **Strategies** enable direct reports to orchestrate their overall plan of attack.

The trick is to know how to go about properly checking these boxes when delegating assignments.

Put the "POW" in emPOWERSment

Periodically engaging in hands-on work with your team can give you opportunities to get to know not just the context within which work is being performed but also how your team members function within this context. Player-managers who think TPL during their situational doing can put a lot of "POW" into their delegations of key assignments. Here's a more detailed look at the *POW* of emPOWERSment:

Proficiency

While engaging in situational doing, can-do leaders can learn the extent to which a person has the basic knowledge, experience, and skills necessary to do a particular assignment properly. As you consider candidates for taking on challenging assignments, ask yourself: What sort of work have I seen this person do in the past that may be somewhat similar to carrying out this new assignment? What experiences will help this person broaden and deepen the expertise we need in our team? Your experience working alongside her may help you decide if she has the skills and experience needed to get the job done well. And, if not, what sort of extra help would she need to get up to speed quickly?

Obligation

Are people actually doing the things you told them to do? Your experience seeing how work is currently being carried out can give you insights both into how work could be better organized and what needs to be emphasized when assigning tasks to improve the likelihood that teammates will do what you want them to focus on. You can also get an idea of who on your team might need more detailed explanations when you delegate assignments.

Willingness

As discussed in chapter 3, to unleash the can-do spirit in others, try to understand what does and does not motivate them. To get a better handle on people's motivational profiles, it's helpful to observe their reactions to different situations and assignments when you are working alongside them. Probe with one or more of the following VITALS questions:

- "What is it about this work that is most meaningful to you?" (Values)
- "What do you find most interesting about this work?" (Interests)
- "Which of your knowledge and skills are making the most difference?" (Talents)
- "What would you like to do in your next few roles?" (Ambitions)
- "What is it about your work that does or does not feel right?" (Longings)
- "What types of people do you most get along with?" (Style)

People cannot always be given the kinds of assignments they want, but the better you understand their VITALS, the more opportunities you'll find to unleash their can-do spirit.

What About "ERS"?

Insights gained from your situational doing can also inform how you can best provide the encouragement, resources, and strategy they need.

Encouragement

Being highly motivated and talented does not, by itself, guarantee that a person will feel confident when confronting a daunting task. "I'm sure you'll do a great job" is certainly a nice thought. But encouragement is often most needed after a person has started working on a tough task. And just providing the cheerleading kind of encouragement won't cut it.

If managers don't personally follow up to find out how things are going after handing out an assignment, they will typically only get feedback from their team if the assignment is going wonderfully or if a terrible problem has occurred. Usually, if things aren't going well, it's too late to get things properly back on track by the time they find out about it.

When you delegate an assignment, schedule regular two-way feedback sessions and be prepared to give instructive advice such as, "You can do this if you make the following adjustments." That kind of encouragement builds real confidence.

Resources

Simply saying, "If you need anything, just let me know," is no guarantee that what is needed to successfully carry out an assignment will be provided. It's your job as manager to figure out in advance what important resources will be needed. Engaging in periodic situational doing increases the odds that as a can-do leader, unlike arms-length managers, you will have a good idea of what's needed to get the job done. If the person to whom you are giving an assignment doesn't have enough arrows in his quiver, you can't expect him to hit all the targets.

Strategies

Direct reports need strategies to orchestrate their overall plan of attack. The person to whom you have given this assignment may have wonderful technical skills and an abundance of resources, but if she doesn't have an overall strategy for making the best use of her skills and resources, she's not likely to be efficient. Working alongside your team members from time to time can enhance your credibility with them when you offer suggestions as to what might work.

It is important to note that this should not be micromanaging. Eliciting a strategy from the person who has been given an assignment is often more motivating than dictating it. Better yet, it's likely to generate some fresh thinking from both of you.

It's useful to remember that if any of the six POWERS described are lacking, your direct report may not have the emPOWERSment needed to get the job done properly. POWERS is a useful checklist. But the question remains—how can these POWERS be brought to the fore when delegating an assignment?

Delegating for Success

Situational doing can certainly give managers a lot of useful background information that can enhance their ability to delegate in ways that set people up to succeed. But what about the delegating process? What's the best way to proceed?

Thinking TPL when delegating an assignment can be a productive way to muster the POWERS to succeed. For example, consider questions focused on the three TPL issues listed in Figure 5-1: Does my team member know what to do? How motivated is my team member? What are my team member's learning gaps?

Figure 5-1. Key TPL Issues to Address When Delegating

How to Think TPL When Delegating an Assignment

The first issue that needs to be tackled when delegating an assignment is communicating a clear idea of what needs to be done (Task). CLEAR is an acronym for clarity, linkages, expectations, authority, and results. You also need to discuss an assignment in ways that relate to the team member's VITALS profile to unleash a strong willingness to do the very best (People). It is also imperative when delegating an important task to determine whether the person has the necessary proficiency to do the assignment properly (Learning). What sort of encouragement might be needed along the way to overcome obstacles and setbacks? The ASPIRE process for identifying and closing learning gaps is described later in this chapter.

Here are the TPL boxes to check when delegating important tasks:

☑ T: Define CLEAR tasks.

☑ P: Check their VITALS.

☑ L: ASPIRE to learn.

How to Avoid Being Skewed When You Are Delegating

Each of us is likely to have particular preferences with regard to dealing with task, people, or learning issues. It's very easy to be skewed when delegating an assignment if certain precautions aren't taken. A manager's natural first move to thinking T, P, or L can dominate how he goes about delegating an assignment, and this can have unfortunate results.

Here's how to bring a balance to the delegating process that gets things done as effectively as possible:

- Know your natural first move for focusing on task, people, or learning issues.
- Take a think TPL power pause prior to beginning the delegation process. This will give you the time to consider the key task, people, and learning issues involved with delegating the assignment.
- Get out of your TPL comfort zone. When delegating, make an effort to properly address the T, P, or L dimension you least prefer.

Some Helpful Reminders When Delegating

The best way for you to make effective use of what follows is entirely up to you. What we've done here is explain in greater detail the acronyms we've created to help you remember the key task, people, and learning issues that are important to consider when delegating a key assignment.

We are not trying to persuade you to memorize all of these acronyms! But we are confident that being mindful of the topics included in these acronyms can help you delegate in a way that successfully musters the POWERS to succeed.

At a minimum, we would suggest that you take a quick look at what follows and see if anything leaps out at you as particularly helpful to remember the next time you delegate an important assignment.

Once you figure out which of the T, P, or L dimensions is your least favorite, we would also suggest that you take a careful look at the section dedicated to that particular dimension. Remembering the acronym associated with your least favorite dimension could help you take a more productive approach to delegating assignments.

Focusing on Task When Delegating

Being CLEAR (clarity, linkages, expectations, authority, and results) can help you remember how to assign tasks in a way that communicates what should be done when given an assignment, including the appropriate strategies and resources.

Clarity

The first step is to clarify the specific goals associated with each task. Provide a clear statement of not only what the person is expected to achieve, but also why the task is being assigned. Your knowledge of the individual's experience level will help you customize your message. Your top priority when assigning goals is to make sure your teammates truly understand what they are meant to achieve. This would be their performance goal. Then you need to specify the parameters of the role associated with the assignment so that the scope of actions and the limits within which to operate are clear. Finally you should discuss any special strategies that might be required.

For example, Pedro, director of operations for an automotive parts distributor, asked Ingrid to cut the time it took to fill customer orders by 30 percent. When stating this goal, Pedro did not dictate how she should get this done. He had recently worked alongside Ingrid and based on his observations he believed she was experienced enough and motivated enough to take on this task.

In addition to explaining what he needed her to achieve, Pedro also explained why he wanted her to perform this task, so that her solutions would be aligned with this larger purpose. He tied the task to the end goal of improving the company's overall customer satisfaction index. Because of his situational doing experience, Pedro also knew that Ingrid was particularly skilled at diplomacy and tact, which would be critical for the success of this assignment. He made sure that Ingrid knew he expected her to put particular emphasis on being diplomatic.

Once Ingrid understood the reason for her new assignment, she made sure that her solution avoided counterproductive things like reassigning people who were currently occupied taking customer orders to working on filling orders. Reducing the number of people available to field customer calls would likely undermine the end goal of improving customer service.

Linkages

In this step you identify key task interdependencies. Make sure that your teammate is aware not only of the critical hand-offs she is expected to make, but also of the key things not under her direct control that need to happen for her to proceed successfully. This way she knows what to monitor, so that she can schedule her own activities accordingly. You also need to identify the key people involved.

For example, Tiffany is a project manager for an engineering services company. Her project team members must interact with stakeholders from many different areas, including sales, engineering design, manufacturing, delivery, installation, and customer support. She knew from her situational doing experiences that some of her team members approached their work "heads down," not considering the implications of their decisions across the organization. So, she made sure they identified the specific stakeholders they needed to connect with, and then required them to check in with these individuals to coordinate handoffs and dependencies. She asked her teammates to identify stakeholders by name, document their relative responsibilities, and indicate any handoff issues that needed to be managed. In some cases, these interactions were with customers. Tiffany also made sure to tell stakeholders and customers to expect to be contacted by one of her team members and why.

Expectations

Consider your risk tolerance for each task before deciding who should be assigned a particular task. How costly are mistakes? If mistakes are made, can recovery occur without major harmful effects? The harder it would be to recover from mistakes, the more careful you need to be when selecting someone to do a high-priority task, and the more vigilant you should be when monitoring the task's execution. You also need to prioritize the assignment and address any unusual features of the situation.

Here's how Lin, a sales manager for a consumer products company, handled the delegation of a high-risk, high-reward assignment. He used his situational doing experience gained by going on joint sales calls with his account executives to determine the capabilities and experience of his team members. When he saw a chance to go after a new sales opportunity with a global distributer, he used this experience to assign the best person for this job.

Lin knew the company would only get one shot at this high-priority opportunity, and the cost of failure was high. So he assigned the work to Tyler, because he believed Tyler had the best mix of experience, assertiveness, and tact. Lin also made sure that Tyler understood how important winning this new account was relative to his other assignments, and that Tyler was expected to manage his time accordingly. Then he reviewed the unique situation surrounding the assignment, including the political and pricing issues the prospective client had had with a previous supplier.

By giving Tyler a heads up, Lin reduced the chance that Tyler would be blindsided by a foreseeable sticky problem, and it gave the two a chance to discuss alternative strategies.

Authority

You'll need to delegate sufficient authority. When you assign someone responsibility for carrying out a task, it is your responsibility to make sure this person has the authority to make decisions, direct people, and make use of appropriate resources. Absent this authority, it is unrealistic to expect a direct report to get the job done.

Specifying the degree of freedom in executing the task is also important. Is this a task that must be done a certain way due to safety or other considerations? Or is this an assignment that can be done any way your direct report wishes, so long as the ultimate goal is achieved?

What is your anticipated level of involvement? Make sure your direct report understands just how involved you expect to be in this project. For example, if you are going to be absorbed in another project, or hard to reach except on certain days, let him know so he can plan accordingly.

Finally, you should let all parties who may be affected by this assignment know, in general terms, what your direct report is doing, and tell them the scope of authority you have delegated. If this is a major assignment or involves a shift in authority relationships, a written communication should be distributed. The announcement phase is a critical stage of the delegation process that is all too often overlooked.

Results

Make sure that the direct report can do the task by analyzing its feasibility. The issue is not whether you could successfully execute this task yourself; rather, can anyone else on your staff reasonably be expected to get the job done right, within the desired timeframe? Your situational doing experience can pay big dividends here.

Avoid nonproductive overloads, however. You may have identified a great person to do an assignment, but what will this do to her work schedule? Before making an assignment, ask yourself: Who is realistically available? Will this assignment be disruptive or cause a nonproductive overload?

For best results, be sure also to establish an assignment timeline and deliverables. Specify not only when the assignment is due to be completed but also the specific times when you expect progress reports. If the assignment includes the creation of some tangible product or products, specify the precise form these should take.

Focusing on People When Delegating

When assignments are being delegated, the VITALS acronym can help a manager use motivators that are likely to increase the team's level of willingness when given an assignment. For example, use positive language that is likely to achieve the best result:

> I think this assignment is a strong match for you. It builds on your strong *interest* in derivatives and your *talent* for problem solving, and gives you the kind of experience you will need to get promoted (*ambition*). You'll have to make good use of your calm and patient *style* to put up with some of the in-your-face personalities you are going to have to deal with, but I know you can step up to the challenge.

Here are some ways you can connect the dots between assignments and what gets your team members motivated.

Values

Create a sense of mission. People tend to work harder to achieve assigned goals when they believe that what they are being asked to do has a level of importance that feels like a mission. At the very least, make sure the person to whom you are giving an assignment understands how getting this task done right contributes to the success of the team. If it's a really important assignment, explain why in a way that is likely to be congruent with an important value held by the recipient of this assignment. Give big reasons for big assignments.

Interests

Encourage participation as much as you can. Enthusiastic acceptance of assignments is often best generated by encouraging your team members to participate as much as possible in the delegation process. The ultimate goal of an assignment may not be negotiable, but many of the particulars of how it will be carried out can be negotiated. As a result, you'll not only get better buy-in, but also better ideas for how to make an assignment work. Because of this added motivation and intelligence, you are likely to get better performance.

Do not continually dump unpleasant tasks on the same person. Every job requires a certain amount of unpleasant work, but unless you are in the construction business, you shouldn't be calling on the same person to dig the dirt. Unless, of course, you are trying to force a resignation.

Talents

Match strengths with opportunities. Whenever there is more than one person to whom you might assign a task, the obvious question is: Which of these candidates has the best skill set to accomplish this task? But your answer should not necessarily determine who gets the assignment. Thinking more broadly and putting this assignment in the context of who should be doing what on your team, your highest priority should be given to putting people's strengths to work where they can have the greatest impact. If, for example, you are trying to decide who should be assigned to fix an annoying but not terribly important computer problem in your office, you probably shouldn't give this assignment to the person with the best computer skills. That person's computer skills would be put to better use helping you create a high-priority proposal for a potentially lucrative client.

Specifically mention particular talents and personal characteristics that make the person you select a good choice for an assignment. Whenever possible, let your choice know why you believe he is a good person to get the job done. Even if he's the only person available at the time, you're likely to get a better performance if you point out a skill that will enable him to do the task successfully. Even saying, "We're in a bind here, I know I can go to you to help us out and you'll give it your best effort," is preferable to saying nothing. Never forget the power of positive expectations.

Don't assign challenging, must-get-it-right tasks to unproven people unless you are willing to keep a very close eye on how the project is progressing. You also need to be prepared to put someone else in charge or step in and do it yourself if things start going badly. Ideally, you want to give high-priority assignments to those you've tested yourself through situational doing. If you don't know the person well, at least get personal references from people you trust, and seek specific evidence of prior accomplishments in similar situations.

Ambitions

Whenever possible, discuss the personal relevance the task has for the person, beyond simply keeping her job. The better you know a person's career ambitions and organizational aspirations, the easier it will be to point out ways in which an assignment will help her advance her career. What if it's an assignment you know she doesn't want to do? In this case, saying something like, "I know this isn't what you have your heart set on, but if we can get this done properly, I'll be in a better position to give you the assignment you really want" may help.

Longings

Everyone has longings for certain things, like achievement, affiliation, power, or autonomy. Think about how the assignment provides opportunities for tapping into these longings and consider who might be the best match.

You should also consider the impact on team morale. Will others on your staff feel passed over or that you are playing favorites? You can't prevent a certain amount of grousing, particularly from staffers who wanted the assignment. However, do whatever you can to keep a negative reaction from getting out of control. If someone you don't think is ready has previously expressed an interest in this kind of assignment, acknowledge his disappointment and tell him what he needs to do to be ready in the future. The personal attention will likely take the edge off his disappointment.

Style

Styles are neither right nor wrong. They simply reflect your customary way of relating to people, processes, details, and challenges. There are many readily available assessment instruments that can give you an insight into your style, including the often-used Myers-Briggs Type Indicator, Hogan Assessments, and the DiSC Assessment. Knowing the preferences and blind spots of your own style will make it easier for you to assess your teammates' styles. While it's often the case that player-managers can't give their team formal, psychometric-style assessments, interacting with them as a situational doer allows the player-manager to observe their preferred ways of communicating, solving problems, making decisions, and dealing with conflict. Knowing how a teammate's style plays out in the context of work will not only help you communicate more effectively with her, but also help you figure out how well her style matches the needs of a task. Some assignments are not a great match for certain styles. For example, a very reserved, detail-oriented person might be a poor fit for an assignment working with a highly assertive, big-picture, Type-A stakeholder.

Focus on Learning When Delegating

It may seem that time spent addressing learning issues is time taken away from actually doing the task. And it often is. But it is also true that time invested up front making sure your team has the learning resources and coaching they need is time you won't have to spend dealing with poorly executed assignments.

Focusing properly on addressing learning issues is a classic case of spending a little time now to save a whole lot of time later on. To get your team properly focused on productive learning, particularly when delegating assignments that are a stretch in terms of their current knowledge and abilities, consider using the six-step ASPIRE coaching process:

1. Assess learning needs.
2. Specify desired learning outcomes.

3. Plan how learning will be achieved.
4. Initiate the learning process.
5. Review the learner's progress.
6. Encourage the learner.

Using the ASPIRE process when you are delegating a stretch assignment can help you create the kind of learning environment that develops needed proficiencies.

Assess

Assessing learning needs means determining what must be learned for people to be able to perform current or future tasks successfully. Use your situational doing knowledge to assess the strengths and learning gaps of your team.

Specify

Specifying desired learning outcomes means stating explicitly what the learner should be able to do as a result of the intended training. It's not always easy for a direct report who is given a challenging new assignment to admit that he has a lot to learn and could use some help. A good way to begin addressing learning issues is to ask, "So that I can get you the help you need, I need to know if there are things you will have to do that you have never done before, or that you have had difficulty with in the past." If the person is not forthcoming, you can suggest some areas where you think he might need help. If you are going to properly address learning issues, it's important to identify what each person needs to learn.

Plan

Planning how learning will be achieved means selecting the method or methods to achieve learning outcomes. You and your team member should form a learning strategy together. Whenever you delegate an assignment that requires significant learning, discuss with your direct report her learning strategy. Ask what her strategy is for learning the key things she needs to learn. If you are not satisfied with her response, make suggestions.

If you believe there are significant learning gaps that could put the assignment at risk, review the learning resources that could be made available to the person who has been assigned the task. Think broadly. Depending upon cost, time, and availability, recommend one or more of the following learning resources: books, articles, videos, workshops, computer-assisted learning programs, examples of previous similar assignments, briefings by people who successfully carried out this kind of assignment, and personal coaching from you. Don't wait for your direct report to ask for help.

Initiate

Initiating the learning process means just that—getting it started. How this should be done depends on the chosen learning method. This could mean helping a team member improve his communication skills to prepare for an important client presentation. Or you could assign a coach or mentor to help bolster a teammate's interpersonal dynamics. However you and the intended learner decide to proceed, proceed you must, or there's no point to the coaching process.

Review

Reviewing the learner's progress should include not only making an assessment of the progress relative to desired learning outcomes, but also having a two-way discussion if things are or are not progressing as hoped.

Be sure to identify things you could do differently to hasten progress. One way to get this conversation going is to ask the learner, "Can you tell me two things: Something I've been doing that's helping you learn and something you wish I would do differently?" You will get a more thoughtful response if you tell your team member in advance that you will be asking these questions.

Use positive-negative feedback where appropriate. When you give corrective feedback it needs to be instructive and offered in the spirit of helping the team get even better. (Chapter 6 covers positive-negative feedback in more detail.)

Encourage

Encouraging the learner—similar to the *E* for encouragement in emPOW-ERSment—means attending to the emotional as well as mental side of learning, particularly when the going gets tough. Encouraging persistence is important. Even if the learning is proceeding as planned, it's important to encourage your team member not to get overconfident and let up. If your teammate is feeling a bit down because the learning's not coming as easily as he had hoped, remind him why he is doing it in the first place, and tell him explicitly, "I know you have the talent to learn this." Great coaches and leaders teach confidence. Similarly, you can reframe setbacks as "learning opportunities."

Offer similar encouragement during stretch assignments. Your situational doing is likely to give you a good sense of when a person does not yet fully have the knowledge, skills, and experience to handle an assignment with ease. When handing out this kind of stretch assignment, you may need to encourage persistence and learning from setbacks along the way.

Further Helpful Reminders When Delegating

OK, did you come up with a task, people, or learning issue that you believe is important, but was missing from the helpful reminders list? If you did, great! You are really starting to think TPL.

Here's another helpful reminder. If something you are delegating is not working out well, ask yourself the following questions and make the appropriate adjustments:

- "Have I fully focused on mustering the POWERS to succeed?"
- "Have I defined and communicated CLEAR tasks?
- "Have I checked the VITALS of my people?
- "Have I helped my people ASPIRE to learn?

We are not suggesting that you attempt to memorize all of these helpful reminders for delegating. But if taking a look at this section gives you a pretty good sense of how to think TPL when delegating, you will be well on your way to mustering the POWERS to succeed!

The CDL Playbook

Use situational doing to inform your delegation. In this way you will get to know not only the context within which work is actually being performed but also how your team members function within this context. This is information that arms-length managers only get second- and thirdhand.

- **Focus on mustering the POWERS to succeed.** The POWERS acronym (proficiency, obligation, willingness, encouragement, resources, and strategy) can help you remember the six qualities associated with a person who is fully empowered to succeed. Think TPL when delegating to muster the POWERS to succeed. Think Task to define CLEAR assignments. Think People to check their VITALS. Think Learning to encourage team members to ASPIRE to learn.

- **Take TPL power pauses to avoid being skewed** when delegating. Know your natural first move and get out of your TPL comfort zone.

- **Assign CLEAR tasks.** The CLEAR acronym (clarity, linkages, expectations, authority, and results) can help you remember how to assign tasks in a way that clearly specifies the obligations, strategies, and resources associated with your delegations.

- **Use the VITALS acronym** (values, interests, talents, ambitions, longings, and style) to help you remember the motivators that are likely to determine the level of willingness your team members feel when given an assignment.

- Use the **ASPIRE acronym** (assess, specify, plan, initiate, review, and encourage) to help you remember how to promote productive learning when delegating.
- **Ask yourself: Have I fully focused on mustering the POWERS to succeed?** If a delegation is not working out well, what adjustments do you need to make?

6

TO KEEP IMPROVING: CREATE A CAN-DO LEARNING CULTURE

In this chapter we will show you how as a can-do leader you will have many on-the-spot opportunities to create a can-do learning culture that inspires continuous improvement.

What Is a Can-Do Learning Culture?

As with all learning cultures, there's a strong commitment to learning. But because the learning that occurs is primarily the product of observing and interacting with people who are actively engaged in getting things done, a true can-do learning culture also includes:

- On-the-spot performance feedback that educates—highly instructive real-time feedback.
- Positive-negative feedback—corrective feedback that inspires continuous improvement.
- Sit-do coaching—in-depth coaching based on situational doing observations and follow through.
- Candid sit-do postmortems—transparent, mutually supportive debriefings that pinpoint accountability for needed improvements in team functioning, and are modeled on the Blue Angels' debriefing sessions.

This chapter looks at how you can be the leader, coach, and role model who makes this happen.

Be Mindful of On-the-Spot Opportunities and Challenges

Your role as a player-manager gives you the opportunity when you are situationally doing to make on-the-spot observations and suggest solutions from both a professional and a managerial perspective. This means you are likely to have many CDL advantages when it comes to giving and getting useful feedback and coaching. You can make firsthand observations that enable you to do the following:

- Assess the effectiveness of techniques used by your team to perform key tasks.
- Identify things that inhibit goal progress that are not under your team members' control, and rectify the situation.
- Identify changes you and your team need to make to better achieve your big picture goals.
- Catch little problems early and do something about them before they become big problems.
- Give and get on-the-spot performance feedback and coaching.

Cory, a manager who led projects in a national change management consulting practice, is good example of a player-manager who learned about the CDL advantage. Cory often led project teams to help his clients manage the people side of large, complex systems integration business transformations. He was a highly competent, hands-on project manager who regularly applied his in-depth expertise in systems integration and change management to his projects. However, Cory was much more into *doing* than *leading*, and as a result he had a reputation for micromanaging, over-controlling, and not developing his team members. When he received his next performance review, Cory was a bit disheartened. But he was also eager to improve. With a little coaching, encouragement, and reinforcement, Cory was well positioned to create a can-do learning environment for his project team.

Cory initially argued that he was too busy doing work himself to find much time to assess and develop his team members. However, after a few coaching sessions, he began to recognize that being a player-manager gave him some on-the-spot opportunities to observe his team in action. He saw that these observations, along with ongoing team discussions, gave him a unique perspective on the strengths and weaknesses of his team members.

For example, Cory created sit-do opportunities to join each of his consultants when they conducted client interviews. He soon discovered that each one was operating in a bit of a silo, and the individual interviews didn't uncover sufficient information about the critical handoffs that needed to be addressed in the new business processes. Cory also observed that his team members did too much telling and not enough open-ended questioning during the interviews. Rather than solving these issues himself, Cory facilitated a team meeting during which the consultants on his team suggested adding focus groups with key stakeholders to identify hand-off issues and communication breakdowns. Cory also took advantage of his sit-do opportunities to coach team members on improving their inquiry skills.

Over time, with some encouragement, Cory began to see the value of using sit-do experiences to provide on-the-spot feedback, coaching, and support, even while he was doing. He continued to say that he felt too busy, but he acknowledged that he was better able to balance his doing and leading.

However, Cory still tended to fall back into the habit of being very directive—telling people what to do versus asking questions, listening, and engaging in co-creating solutions for day-to-day issues. He needed to be reminded that the leadership effect never stops (LENS), and the things he did and didn't do while working alongside his team members tended to get magnified in their eyes. He began to see that his behavior was actually inhibiting growth and development, because his team was waiting for him to solve problems and make the decisions. While Cory wanted to create a learning culture, the first step he needed to take was to change his own behaviors and improve:

- How he gave feedback and coaching, especially his nonverbal communication. After some coaching, Cory was able to tell when he was about to show impatience. He began working to clear his mind and focus on asking good questions and carefully listening to the responses. He saw almost immediate benefits from engaging his team members in a dialogue and having a thoughtful two-way conversation about performance.

- How he reacted to the feedback and coaching he got from his team—body language included. Although Cory asked for feedback, he often got defensive and tried to justify his actions. However, after some coaching he realized that this behavior discouraged people from speaking—he learned to say "thank you for the feedback, what else?"

Cory discovered that having a LENS also gave him many on-the-spot opportunities to be an influential can-do learning role model.

Take TP&L Power Pauses

Yes, you saw it right, TP&L. It's not a typo! It's a type of thinking that will help you focus on identifying learning opportunities when you are giving and getting performance feedback.

When you are engaged in situational doing it is very easy to get so caught up in the pressures of the moment that the learning dimension gets scant attention when giving on-the-spot feedback. Simply saying to yourself, "Think TP&L," can help you remember to put a proper focus on giving instructive performance feedback.

Here are some of the key task, people, and learning issues to bear in mind so that your performance feedback triggers high levels of performance.

Key Task Issues

Be sure that you are giving feedback that is relevant to achieving important tasks. Before launching into giving performance feedback, ask yourself, is this task likely to have a significant impact on achieving both team and organizational goals? To maintain an appropriate focus on task demands and task-oriented behaviors when you are giving feedback, be sure to identify tasks that have to be successfully performed to achieve key goals.

Drawing on your position and perspective as team leader, consider:

- What tasks must we excel at today?
- What feedback have we received about our task performance?
- What future tasks must we be prepared for?

When appropriate, you might also want to solicit feedback from your manager, clients, team, and people in your professional network to make sure you and your team are focused on the most important things from their perspective.

Key People Issues

Relevant people issues need to be addressed to encourage recipients of your feedback to be receptive to what you have to say and to act on this information with commitment, not resentment. You can never be sure how people will receive your feedback, but properly attending to the following issues will improve the chances that they will listen to what you have to say and act on the information in a positive way:

- Consider your team members' VITALS. Obviously, you can't know everything about their VITALS profiles, but the more you know, the better your feedback will be.
- Be a "font" not a "fire hydrant." As a general rule, less is often more when giving feedback. You may have a lot of great improvement ideas, but if you dump them all at once they'll land like a ton of bricks. Focus on a few specific behaviors and you'll get better results. The last thing you want is for your team members to resent your presence because you are "always spouting off better ways to do things."

Key Learning Issues

Because instructive feedback is most likely to lead to performance improvement, top priority should be given to facilitating learning during feedback discussions. To provide your team members with feedback that educates, do the following things:

- Give accurate feedback as soon as it can be profitably absorbed. On-the-spot feedback sessions, in response to something that your team member did recently, are more likely to facilitate learning than annual reviews where you mention for the first time something that happened five months ago.
- Explain the "whys." Performance feedback is most instructive if recipients can learn not only what is and is not working for them, but also why.
- When giving praise, be specific. What exactly were the positive effects associated with the actions they took? When team members do something well, tell them specifically what they have done well. People are likely to keep doing the things they are recognized for doing.
- Provide opportunities and encouragement for team members to seek feedback from many different sources. Soliciting feedback from the people who are stakeholders in the success of the projects you are engaged in (such as peers, clients, and other managers) can provide your team with perspectives on what they need to learn that they are likely to find useful. It can also provide motivation to improve performance that goes beyond simply trying to please and placate their boss. Encourage your team to actively seek feedback from many different sources, with questions like, "What sort of feedback have you been able to get on your performance?" and, "Are you getting the same message concerning your performance on this project from different sources?"
- Do not focus too much on what you would have done. This is all too easy to do during feedback sessions. Instead, ask questions that clarify the positive or negative effects that their approach is having. Remind yourself that feedback sessions are best when the communication and learning is two-way.
- Make sure your team member understands the feedback. Ask for her version of your message with a question like, "Just to be sure we're on the same page, how would you sum up what's been discussed?"

- Use feedback to initiate action. It may be very instructive, but if your feedback is not acted on, what use is it? Your team members must learn to take action in response to receiving useful feedback. To encourage this, ask questions like: "What will you do now that you have learned this?" "When are you going to begin?" "How will you collect feedback on your development?" "When shall we review your progress?"

- Get feedback on your feedback. Maybe you have it all wrong—perhaps you've either overlooked or misunderstood something about your team member's situation. If you want your team member to be responsive to your feedback, it's a good idea to listen carefully to what he has to say about the accuracy and quality of your feedback. If he is not forthcoming, ask in a nonchallenging tone, "Is this feedback helpful? Or is there something important that I am overlooking here?" You might learn something.

This is not an all-inclusive list of every task, people, and learning issue that might prove important when giving learning-centered performance feedback. But it should be enough to get you thinking TP&L when giving feedback. If you put particular emphasis on the L, you are likely to deliver task-relevant feedback that's highly instructive. This is the kind of feedback that can empower significant performance improvement, but only if it is presented and received in a way that is motivating.

Go for Positive-Negative Feedback

Positive-negative may seem like an oxymoron, but consider this: Say you want to get better at golf. How long would you continue to take lessons from a golf pro who only told you what you were doing well? How useful is only getting positive feedback?

Whatever our interest or hobby might be, when we are not at work we are willing to pay good money for negative feedback about our performance—provided that this feedback makes us believe that if we make some adjustments we can improve our performance.

Simply put, the hallmark of a true can-do learning culture is an environment where the vast majority of participants aspire to get the kind of negative performance feedback that makes them feel positive about their chances of continuing to get even better in the future.

As a can-do leader, you are not some coach your team members hired to help them get better at something. And, as we mentioned earlier, subordinates can feel very threatened by negative comments about their current performance when they come from The Boss. So, you need a strategy for delivering corrective feedback in a way that actually makes your teammates feel good about their ability get better. Here's a strategy that can help you do just that.

Be a Role Model for Turning Negatives Into Positives

Demonstrate that you want to receive corrective feedback that is instructive. Your team members are likely to be much more open to giving and getting corrective performance feedback if they see how enthusiastic you are about getting their suggestions for how you can improve as their leader. When you ask for feedback, ask for specifics. For example, "Could you tell me two things I'm doing well as your manager and two areas where you think I could use some improvement?" Or you could ask about a specific project: "What could I have done differently to manage the Cambridge account better?" If a team member seems reluctant to respond, tell her you'd really appreciate it if she could think about it and that you'll check back with her later for a response. Then, be sure to follow up.

Remember, the leadership effect never stops. You are under the LENS! If you want people to be willing to give and receive corrective feedback that is instructive, you have to be ready, willing, and able to receive it yourself. When you show you are a leader who thrives on receiving performance-enhancing feedback, you set the stage for your team being willing to give it a try. Follow the golden rule: Respond to feedback from others, as you would have them respond to your feedback. You should also be a role model for how negative feedback should be received by taking it well yourself. If you are feeling very defensive (or simply don't have time to respond):

- Thank your team member for her candor.
- Make an appointment with her to discuss this further.
- And, keep it.

When you meet again, find something useful in what she told you, using phrases like "that's a useful improvement opportunity for me," or "thanks, that will be a good learning opportunity for me." At the very least, compliment her for being candid about what she believes to be an important issue. Show that you've thought about her feedback and repeat what she said to you, using her words as much as possible. Give an honest response and be specific about what you will or will not do as a result. Any desired adjustments you make in response to feedback will be noticed and appreciated.

To turn negatives into positives when giving performance feedback consider the question: "Educate or assassinate?" Before giving corrective feedback, it's a good idea to examine your motivations, especially if you are worked up because this person didn't do what you wanted. If you feel like lashing out, it's best to pause and wait until you've calmed down. Then ask yourself, "Do I want to hurt this person or help this situation?" If your answer is the latter, determine the specific behavior or behaviors you want to encourage or eliminate, and focus on giving feedback that educates. Be careful about buying into the proverbial "feedback sandwiches," however. This is the idea that whenever you give corrective feedback you have to say something nice about the recipient before and after giving the tough feedback. Positive-negative feedback is different. It is a matter of explaining what is actually very positive about the corrective feedback you are offering.

Use reframing to turn negatives into positives. Managers typically feel uncomfortable when pointing out shortcomings of a direct report's performance. Reframe the mistake as an opportunity to make an adjustment that will make your team member more successful.

When offering corrective feedback, try sprinkling in phrases like:

- Here's something I think will really help you . . .

- I think you can get even better in your current role if . . .
- Can I tell you something that I think could make you really amazing at . . .

To show how important you believe giving and getting instructive corrective feedback is to continuous performance improvement, avoid using negative descriptions when giving your feedback. Focus instead on the opportunity to make positive improvements. Get in the habit of using upbeat terms like *improvement opps* and *learning opps* when discussing adjustments that you would like to see made. Using a positive tone of voice and body language also sends the unmistakable message that you are making an earnest attempt to help them improve.

Praise positive responses to corrective feedback. There are, of course, times when behavior that is clearly unacceptable occurs and must be addressed immediately. And if someone is failing to make agreed-to changes in his performance, that can't be ignored either. But if you want to encourage an eagerness to engage in corrective feedback, it's helpful to provide positive follow-ups on corrective feedback you have given. Whenever you ask someone to make an adjustment in performance, make a point to compliment performance improvements in a timely fashion. You should also be specific when you give these compliments. While we tend to repeat what we've been recognized for doing, it helps if we know with some precision what we are being rewarded for. Point out some of the specific positive effects and, whenever possible, relate them to the overall function of the team.

Encourage Sit-Do Coaching

Sit-do coaching is typically initiated by a can-do leader's situational doing observations, but it can also include the following features:

- off-site coaching prompted by on-site performance observations
- direct reports coaching their manager
- on-site coaching that reinforces off-site training.

The learning that occurs through sit-do coaching can add depth to instructive feedback. Here are some strategies you can use to enhance your sit-do coaching.

Be the Big Picture Coach for Your Team

To set the stage for your participation in sit-do coaching in a way that creates and reinforces a can-do learning culture, do the following:

Provide "sightlines" to the big picture. Don't assume it's ever enough to only describe the vision and mission for your team just once. When you are engaged in situational doing, take advantage of the fact that you are well positioned to provide on-the-spot sightlines to the big picture. Explain how what they are currently working on relates to satisfying the needs of the people who will use your team's products or services.

The better your teammates understand how what they've been assigned to do can affect the achievement of your team's most important end goals, the more likely they will be to commit to continuously learning how to get better. And the more open they are likely to be to giving and getting performance feedback and coaching.

Demonstrate the importance you place on learning from one another to keep getting better and better as a team. It's not enough to simply state this belief; you need to show it. Set the example by asking for a half hour or so of coaching from team members from time to time so that you can keep up-to-date with what's happening in their areas of specialization. And be an attentive student.

Use Coaching With ASPIRE to Learn

To get your team focused on productive learning, consider using the ASPIRE to learn coaching process described in chapter 5:

1. Assess learning needs.
2. Specify desired learning outcomes and their expected impact.
3. Plan how learning will be achieved.
4. Initiate the learning process.
5. Review the learner's progress.
6. Encourage the learner.

Kelly is the training director for a regional bank. Here's how she made good use of the ASPIRE to learn process. She has 12 direct reports who range from very seasoned to somewhat experienced but new to the company. She and her team are responsible for designing, developing, and facilitating functional training programs to prepare their in-house "clients"—tellers and supervisors—to address a wide variety of banking needs in an environment where the technology is constantly upgrading.

To be effective as training business partners, Kelly's team needed to be responsible for a wide range of activities, including conducting interviews and focus groups to understand their clients' learning needs; designing instructional e-modules, virtual sessions, and classroom training; and facilitating these sessions. This all happened in an environment where systems and processes were in continuous flux. Kelly and her team needed cross training to make sure that each team member was able to do whatever was needed to get the work done.

Kelly, as a player-manager, often found herself conducting interviews and focus groups, briefing bank managers, and co-designing training. And given her strong background in e-learning, she also developed engaging e-modules and webinars.

Max, one of Kelly's direct reports, was an experienced instructional designer who was new to the bank. He had come from a siloed environment, where instructional designers took direction from training managers, and he was accustomed to designing programs without much client interaction. While situational doing, Kelly observed that Max didn't have much experience conducting interviews and focus groups—tasks he needed to perform well to become a successful training business partner. Kelly used the six steps of ASPIRE coaching process to help Max become a higher-performing member of her team.

First she *assessed* the learning needs. This meant determining what Max needed to learn to become a successful training business partner. While situational doing and conversing with him, Kelly observed Max's current job performance and started to get a sense of his VITALS profile. She asked him what he thought he needed to learn to do now that he was in a new job so he could become a full training business partner. Kelly knew that it was important that Max take ownership of the specific things he needed to learn.

Next Kelly *specified* desired learning outcomes. This meant stating explicitly what Max should be able to do differently as a result of the intended learning. Kelly knew Max needed to understand the specific outcomes and demonstrated actions that would indicate that the desired learning had occurred. She helped Max think about observable behaviors he would be expected to demonstrate as a result of the training, including being able to conduct diagnostic interviews, facilitate interactive focus groups, prepare a targeted needs assessment, organize a development plan, communicate and collaborate effectively with his clients, and be able to successfully manage conflict when necessary. And finally, Kelly helped Max envision the expected improvements for him, his clients, and the success of the bank if he could demonstrate the intended learning.

The next step was *planning* how learning would be achieved. Kelly selected learning methods she thought would help Max by asking him, "What's the best way for you to learn these kind of things?" She knew that getting Max involved in the process was also likely to be a great motivator. They decided on a mix of stretch job assignments, several targeted e-readings, and a relationship-building training seminar. Kelly also assigned a co-worker to mentor Max, and she planned to act as Max's on-the-spot coach. They also agreed on milestones where progress would be reviewed.

Initiating the learning process for Max depended on the learning methods they chose. Kelly got approval for Max to attend a virtual training session, and she coached Max on specific relationship behaviors. She also gave Max a stretch assignment that required him to conduct a needs assessment with a group of tellers, and she assigned Doreen, an experienced training business partner, as Max's mentor. Kelly also searched her files and identified a few specific readings she thought Max would find helpful.

Reviewing the learner's progress meant that Kelly set up regular check-ins to make sure that Max was making progress. Kelly not only provided on-the-spot performance feedback, but also scheduled regular coaching sessions to assess progress, discuss successes, and share positive-negative feedback. Kelly paid particular attention to identifying the things they could both do differently to hasten progress. One way she got this conversation going was to ask Max, "Can you tell me two things: Something

I've been doing that's helping you learn and something you wish I would do differently?" She told Max in advance that she would be asking these questions because she knew he would give a more thoughtful response if he had time to think about what he wanted to say.

Encouraging the learner meant Kelly needed to pay attention to the emotional side of learning. Even though Max's learning was proceeding as planned, Kelly believed it was important to encourage Max not to get overconfident and stop working hard. When Max was feeling a bit down because he was struggling to manage difficult conversations with a demanding stakeholder, Kelly reminded him why and how what he was doing would help him get better and better in the future. Based on her sense of Max's VITALS, Kelly told him, "Given your talent for problem solving and your ambition to be promoted in the future, I know you will keep getting better and better at this."

The ASPIRE acronym helped Kelly remember the things she could do to get properly focused on the process of facilitating productive learning. Let's take a look now at a well-proven strategy you can use to elicit candid performance-enhancing feedback during post-event debriefing sessions with your team.

Conduct Candid Sit-Do Postmortem Feedback Sessions

Have you ever seen the U.S. Navy's Blue Angels flight demonstration squadron perform breath-taking high-in-the sky close-formation maneuvers? How do they do it, again and again, under such challenging conditions?

It's easy to understand that the slightest error by any of the six elite navy and marine pilots in command of these F/A-18 Hornet aircraft—often flying in tight diamond formation at speeds of 400 miles per hour or more and only 36 inches apart—could have devastating consequences.

What you may not know, though, is that the way the Blue Angels conduct their post-event debriefing sessions immediately after each seemingly odds-defying Blue Angel flight performance is equally stunning. Although we will likely never fly like the Blues, we can learn something from how they provide feedback to one another in their post-performance sessions.

The Blues' debrief process is based on the idea that protecting and enhancing the safety of the team can only occur if every person is honest, transparent, and candid about what went right and wrong. As the pilots enter the debriefing room, they leave their "rank" at the door and operate as peers working toward a common goal of continuous learning. Each Blue Angel feedback debrief starts with the leader setting the tone by admitting "safeties"—candidly confessing to mistakes he made during flight maneuvers—no matter how minor. He thereby opens himself up to criticism from the rest of the team before commenting on any mistakes made by others.

The other pilots then each take a turn admitting mistakes they made and discussing mistakes that they observed others making. They also talk about what they will do to fix the mistakes they've made. It is customary for each person to end with a loud and clear "glad to be here" expression of commitment, trust, and respect for the team. During these team-focused debriefings, it is perfectly acceptable and completely expected that even the most junior pilot respectfully critiques the most senior pilot's actions, without hesitation or fear of retribution.

Imagine if your organization had a similar sit-do postmortem where everyone, regardless of seniority or title, felt comfortable sharing direct, candid feedback in the spirit of continuous learning? Blue Angel–style feedback sessions could pinpoint accountability for needed improvements in team functioning. Done well these debriefings can generate the kind of candor that both guards against escalating breakdowns in team performance and also guides team members in the direction of continuous improvement.

When as a player-manager you are working alongside your teammates on various assignments you will have opportunities as you reach milestones to conduct candid postmortem feedback sessions. As a can-do leader who is mindful of what needs to be done to create a can-do learning culture, you will be well positioned to conduct postmortems that elicit public commitments to take responsibility for productive adjustments in how your team functions.

When you conduct a sit-do postmortem, be sure to lead off with a personal "improvement opp" you need to attend to. It is also a good idea to end the sessions positively by, for example, saying something like, "I really enjoy having the opportunity to work and learn with all of you."

And it is very likely you will enjoy these opportunities to work alongside your team if you create the kind of learning culture that encourages everyone to be open to giving and getting positive-negative feedback.

The CDL Playbook

To create a can-do learning culture that continually builds your team's capacity be sure to make good use of the following strategies:

- **Be mindful of your on-the-spot opportunities and challenges:**
  - You will have many opportunities while you are *situationally doing* to give and get performance-enhancing feedback and coaching. But because you are The Boss how you do this will be magnified by your LENS.
  - Use your LENS to create a can-do learning culture by being a role model for the approach you would like your teammates to use when giving and getting feedback and coaching.
- **Take TP&L power pauses:**
  - To make sure you are giving the right kind of performance feedback, take TP&L power pauses to remind yourself to give highly instructive feedback, rather than vague or negative feedback.

- **Go for positive-negative feedback:**
  - Be a role model for turning negatives into positives by emphasizing the positive improvement opportunities that can come with accepting and acting on corrective feedback.
  - Praise performance improvements that result from acting on corrective feedback.
  - Make a point of demonstrating that you want to *receive* corrective feedback by thanking anyone who gives it to you.
  - Act on feedback you receive or give good reasons for not doing so.
- **Encourage sit-do coaching:**
  - Be the big picture coach for your team.
  - Solicit coaching from your team. And take it well.
  - Use the ASPIRE to learn coaching process.
- **Conduct candid sit-do postmortem feedback sessions:**
  - Hold Blue Angel–style post-event debriefings that set aside rank and seniority.
  - Pinpoint accountability for needed improvements in team functioning.
  - Promote candor by leading off with an improvement opp that you believe you need to attend to.
  - End the debriefing with an expression of how much pleasure you take in being able to both work and learn with your team.

7

TO BE A STAR WITH CAREER SECURITY: BE A CAN-DO CHAMPION

In the process of becoming a can-do leader, a player-manager can become a can-do champion, and map out a personally satisfying and highly rewarding career path. This chapter shares some strategies you can use to become a star in your field and have some fun in the process.

In recent years many managers who have let their technical and functional skills atrophy to the point where they no longer have a distinct area of value-adding professional expertise have been among the first to be let go during economic downturns. And they are not having an easy time finding new jobs in the increasingly cost-conscious, knowledge-driven work world. Job security is very unlikely to make a comeback in the 21st century, but how about career security? Player-managers who become can-do champions are well positioned for career security because they continue to develop themselves and their network of contacts in ways that enhance their employability.

How to Build Your Brand as a Can-Do Champion

You can become a star in your field and have professional security if you pursue the following three career strategies:

- Continue to develop your professional self in personally meaningful ways that enhance your versatility and strengthen your professional presence and judgment.
- Be a can-do champion whenever you can—that's your brand—in your vertical, horizontal, and diagonal relationships inside and outside your organization.
- Keep adding can-do items to your career portfolio that demonstrate your can-do mindset and accomplishments.

Here's how to pursue these strategies and become a star in the process.

Continue to Develop Your Professional Self

Becoming a manager who continues to develop a distinct area of professional expertise is a great career strategy for maintaining your employability. Being professional, as both a leader and a doer, will give you the ability to continue to add value in many different scenarios.

Set High Goals for Being Professionally Current and Relevant

You must never forget how important it is to continue to develop your professional credentials when you take on a player-manager position, not only to enhance your versatility as a doer, but also to reinforce your competencies, influence, and impact as a leader. It is important not to think like an individual contributor when you consider your personal professional development commitments and needs. Instead, elevate your thinking about what it means to be a highly relevant professional as a can-do leader. Here are some things to think about:

- Graduate from focusing on being a highly competent technical specialist to becoming a highly competent leader with strong professional knowledge and skills.
- Be more selective with regard to the highly specialized technical work you choose to keep your hand in, as discussed in chapter 4. Focus, that is, on doing technical work that will provide the most impact to your organization, your team and, whenever feasible, your own professional brand.

- Focus less on developing narrow how-to technical or functional skills, and more on developing a broad knowledge of when, where, and how these skills can be most usefully deployed in your field.

- Recognize and use your CDL sweet spot for creativity. Can-do leaders have many opportunities to think of new ideas when engaging in situational doing. The leading and doing overlap provides a sweet spot for creativity. Being in the fray in a way that allows you to experience issues firsthand with your team can give you and your staff opportunities to identify new things to achieve and brainstorm innovative solutions.

- Pay particular attention to emerging technologies and skills that might prove useful in your field.

- Become knowledgeable with regard to how skills and techniques evolving in your own field can contribute to addressing broader organizational and societal challenges. For example, an architect might keep up with how certain design strategies could make significant contributions to environmental sustainability.

- Learn how specialists in your own field can productively draw on expertise provided by specialists from different fields. For example, physicians consult with psychologists to develop better strategies for getting patients to take their medications.

Use Your VITALS Profile to Motivate Your Professional Growth

As shown in chapter 5, given your leadership responsibilities as a player-manager, there will be many situations where it is better for your team if you delegate work that you might have liked to do yourself. But having a clear sense of the things you need to do to continue to feel fulfilled as you grow professionally will inform your can-do leader decisions in productive ways—as long as you use the guidelines set forth in the sit-do protocol, that is. To find the right way to define how you really want to grow professionally, it is helpful to identify your VITALS-derived motivators that fit the following categories:

- **Must have.** These would be your key professional interests, talents, and ambitions. They are what motivate your professional growth and define who you are, professionally speaking. You may not always have these activities in your professional mix, but you should seek them out whenever possible. These will likely be the distinct areas of value-adding professional expertise that you can readily deploy while situationally doing.
- **Like to have.** These are things you would like to see in your professional mix, if possible. Perhaps it's a skill you think might be good to develop for future use, or maybe some interests you would like to pursue when you can. But these like-to-haves are not a defining aspect of your professional identity.
- **Not particularly important.** You may have real talents and skills that you would list in this category, but these are areas of minimal professional interest to you. They are not necessary for you to pursue to maintain your professional presence and continuing employability.

Use the CDL Advantage to Stay Current

Use your leadership position to leverage your learning. Here's how:

- Assign staff to learn about things you want to know more about. And then have them brief you.
- Get coached in an area you want to learn more about while engaged in situational doing.
- Actively solicit high-end professional invitations. Because of your role as a leader you can ask to serve on association committees and panels that are professionally informative and that generate access to leaders in your field.
- Seek high-profile assignments and projects. Leading a team of professionals enables you to take on bigger stretch projects than you could as an individual contributor. As the size, scope, and impact of the projects you lead grows, you will increasingly be viewed as an important leader in your field.

- Take advantage of high-level networking opportunities with leaders in other fields. Becoming an effective can-do leader can increase your visibility, not only in your own profession, but also among the leaders of other professions. Accepting invitations to provide advice on high-level, cross-functional committees and boards can generate contacts that keep you apprised of what's going on in the upper levels of allied fields, as well as bring to your attention high-level career opportunities.

Use the knowledge that you gain from pursuing these strategies to set further professional goals for yourself that will give you a feeling of professional fulfillment and continue to enhance your employability.

Be a Can-Do Champion Whenever You Can

When you behave like a can-do champion you are, in effect, being your brand. And if you do this well people will think of you as the kind of person who can get the right things done without a lot of fuss—a reputation that is likely to net you many attractive opportunities throughout your career. Here's what's involved:

- A can-do champion makes a point of always projecting a can-do attitude. In the things that they say and the actions that they take, can-do champions leave no doubt that they are focused on doing whatever it takes to get the right things done. But, of course, that by itself is not enough. You have to be able to back this up.
- A can-do champion builds a can-do culture. Your fastest and surest route to can-do leader stardom is not a relentless focus on building a boss-dependent cult. Focus instead on developing a can-do learning culture that encourages everyone on your team to develop in ways that help them assume greater responsibilities. Be a champion, not for yourself, but for taking a "we-can-do" approach with your team.

That said, developing your reputation as a high-profile professional and leader involves more than just being an effective team leader:

- A can-do champion develops a can-do network on many levels. A can-do network is an extensive, multilevel network of people both inside and outside your organization. Think of these productive relationships as forming the nodes of your career safety net, because when you need help these are the people who are likely be there for you. Your boss, people in top management, and the people who report to you are often important members of your formal can-do network. Making yourself useful to a wide range of people outside your direct line of authority at different levels in your organization can also pay big dividends when you need help getting things done.

- A can-do champion also develops a reputation for being effective and helpful beyond her immediate organization. Developing a can-do reputation with your informal network outside your organization is particularly important from a career security and professional visibility point of view. Professional peers, fellow board members, and other well-placed people you make yourself useful to from time to time can become key contacts for career advancement and security.

- A can-do champion continually nurtures his can-do network. You've no doubt noticed that the way you treat people can have a strong effect on how they treat you. Sociologists call this phenomenon the "norm of reciprocity." It is a good thing to remember when you are focused on nurturing the relationships in your can-do network.

Advice From One of History's Great Can-Do Champions

As a general rule, it's a good idea to offer some help before asking someone for a favor. However, an interesting exception to this give-before-you-get strategy for nurturing relationships was provided by Benjamin Franklin. Franklin had a worldwide reputation for getting all sorts of things done and was a successful practitioner of getting a favor before giving one. When confronted early in his career with an influential new legislator who had resisted his reappointment as clerk of the Pennsylvania General Assembly, instead of "paying any servile Respect to him" to win him over, Franklin took another approach, which he described as follows:

> Having heard that he had in his Library a certain very scarce and curious Book, I wrote a Note to him, expressing my Desire of perusing that Book, and requesting he would do me the Favour of lending it to me for a few Days. He sent it immediately; and I return'd it in about a Week, with another note expressing strongly my Sense of the Favour. When we next met in the House he spoke to me, (which he had never done before) and with great Civility. And he ever after manifested a Readiness to serve me on all Occasions, so that we became Friends, and our Friendship continu'd unto his Death. This is another Instance of the Truth of an old Maxim I had learnt, which says, He that has once done you a Kindness will be more ready to do you another, than he whom you yourself have obliged. (Franklin 2003, 171-172)

Of course, this wasn't a random favor that Franklin requested. Clearly Franklin, who was himself an author and printer, figured out that this influential new member of the assembly shared his strong interest in books and took particular pride in his talent for being able to recognize and acquire interesting examples of the printed word. In other words, this favor was very much in line with Franklin's assessment of this person's VITALS, so to speak.

We may not have Franklin at our side to help us figure out how best to nurture positive relationships with the people we'd like to add to our can-do network, but we do have the think TPL and check their VITALS strategies.

Thinking TPL and Checking VITALS Are Champion Strategies for Networking

For starters, thinking TPL when talking to people we want to include in our network can help us remember to try to find out the following things:

- Task?
  - What are the important goals we share?
  - What are the key tasks that this person seems to be most concerned about?
  - Is there an overlap with tasks that I need to address?

- People?
  - What kind of a person am I dealing with? (More on this in a moment under VITALS.)
  - What can I do to strengthen our current relationship?
  - How receptive might this person be to positive-negative feedback?
- Learning?
  - What important knowledge and skills does this person have?
  - What kinds of things could we learn from each other?

It is also very useful to know how people are skewed in terms of the importance they give to talking about task, people, and learning issues. With regard to checking their VITALS, try to figure out each person's particular values, interests, talents, ambitions, longings, and style. Are there areas of overlap with your key VITALS? Do they appear to have a particular longing for power, affiliation, or achievement? What is their preferred communication style? Would they prefer verbal updates on things of mutual interest or emails with links?

You are not going to have a thorough knowledge of each person's VITALS motivators. And it may take a while to figure out their natural first move on T, P, or L issues. But using these acronyms to help you learn what you can about the important people in your professional network will make it much easier for you to nurture your can-do relationships.

Keep Adding Can-Do Items to Your Career Portfolio

What's a career portfolio? Well, you've found the right executive coaches to ask this particular question. One of the authors of this book also happens to be the senior author of *The Career Portfolio Workbook*!

A career portfolio is a collection of documents and other easily portable artifacts that you can use to validate claims you make about yourself. Having an impressively targeted portfolio is useful not just for getting jobs, but also for getting favorable performance reviews, raises, promotions, and consulting assignments; making desired lateral moves within your organization; and even for changing your career.

Your professional knowledge, skills, and experience are certainly important. But once you are perceived as being sufficiently qualified, employers and potential clients are most likely to pay attention to your personal characteristics and your accomplishments.

This is good news if you are a player-manager who becomes a can-do leader. Having the can-do mindset positions you quite nicely to display can-do personal characteristics that are typically highly valued by employers and clients—namely, being dependable and having a history of taking the initiative to get things done properly with a sense of urgency.

As a can-do leader, you are likely to be able to present impressive examples of your commendable can-do accomplishments. Collecting copies of documents and other items that you can use in interviews for a new job, a raise, or a promotion to verify your can-do mindset and accomplishments can help you keep moving forward in your career. Here's what's involved:

Collect Evidence of Your Can-Do Mindset

Save electronic copies of communications thanking you for your help getting something done. Most useful are images of emails, texts, social media items, handwritten notes—any communication you receive that thanks you for being the kind of person who could be trusted to get a difficult task done. Or it could simply be a note that doesn't refer specifically to your personal qualities, but does make very positive reference to the kind of help you gave them. A note that would give you the opportunity to say to an interviewer, "Here's a nice example of a time I showed a lot of (can-do) initiative and dependability." A favorable annual performance review that commends you for your can-do qualities is also well worth setting aside for potential use in your can-do career portfolio.

Ask grateful people you have helped to email you a quick thank you note for your portfolio. If you've given someone help that demonstrates you are a dependable go-to person, it's typically not inappropriate when they thank you orally to make this "portfolio request." Odds are she will be fascinated to learn that you have a can-do career portfolio. And, once she learns what it is, she may want to know if she should be creating one, too. (Fortunately, you'll have in mind a book or two for her to read.)

Ask people to recommend you or endorse your skills on a business-oriented social networking service like LinkedIn. If you feel comfortable doing so, ask people to go to your LinkedIn page and comment on the value you brought to them.

Use these items to make your can-do intangibles feel more tangible. Your commendable can-do personal characteristics aren't something that can be directly seen or touched. But being able to share documents that praise your can-do qualities can make your can-do persona seem very tangible to an interviewer, boss, or a potential client. If the documents are too personal or confidential to leave with them, that's OK. Just being able to show an image of a thank-you note you received is a powerful way to make your intangibles feel more real.

Keep Filling Your Can-Do Career Portfolio With STARs

In addition to collecting commendations you have received, it's also useful to collect documents and scan images of other items that illustrate some aspect of significant can-do accomplishments that you and your team have had.

Evaluate your can-do accomplishments in terms of their STAR quality. STAR is an oft-used acronym that provides a useful structure for describing your accomplishments:

- **Situation:** challenges, problems, or opportunities that you addressed
- **Task:** what you had to get done
- **Action(s):** the key decisions and actions you and your team took
- **Results:** what you ultimately were able to achieve with your team.

Examples of the kinds of documents that give evidence of your can-do accomplishments include awards you received for accomplishments; news articles about something you and your team accomplished; photographs of you and your team on the web or in newspapers, magazines, or in-house publications because of an accomplishment; sales reports documenting your success; a section from a business plan you created (with proprietary information deleted); and customer satisfaction reports.

Using the STAR method can help you remember how best to describe these accomplishments to an interviewer, boss, or client.

Focus on including accomplishments that are impressive in your field. For example, if you are a national sales manager, evidence of your having found a way to help your team open up productive new accounts shows a highly significant accomplishment in your chosen field. Create a document that lists high-performing new accounts (names deleted to protect proprietary information) that you and your team opened during your first year as national sales manager, along with the percentage increase that these new accounts contributed to overall sales.

Include, if possible, items that illustrate successful innovations generated by your situational doing. As noted earlier, can-do leaders have many opportunities to come up with new ideas when engaging in situational doing. Evidence of something you and your team created while working together—such as pictures of new products, logos, promotional materials, or announcements of new services you and your team developed—can be impressive examples of your can-do ability to innovate as a professional who is also a leader.

Use networking to identify gaps in your current can-do career portfolio. Shoptalk with other upwardly mobile professionals in your field can give you a good idea of what you can add to your portfolio, as well as the areas you need to develop to enhance your employability and fulfill your career ambitions.

Having a can-do career portfolio can help you present yourself not only to a boss, but also to potential employers and clients in a way that demonstrates that you are the kind of professional they'd like to have on their team.

If you are going on a face-to-face interview, consider showcasing your collection of relevant portfolio items as hard copies (in sheet protectors in a thin binder), rather than electronically on your tablet. Being able to touch a document often makes its contents seem more tangible.

Consider creating a digital portfolio you can post on a personal website. However, one cautionary note: Don't include a personal note from someone without permission in a web-based career portfolio. Also be mindful that you will lose control of what gets looked at, and lose the ability to tailor your descriptions of the items in it to the needs of the moment.

Keep a list of your can-do star accomplishments, even if you do not have a portfolio. You do not need to have a "can-do portfolio" to be a can-do champion, but keeping a list of the impressive things you have done as a can-do leader can be very helpful when you are preparing a resume or going on an interview.

Establish your brand as a can-do champion and the future is yours. Have fun, and please tell us about it. And who knows, you might very well end up in our next book!

The CDL Playbook

- **Continue to develop your professional self** in ways that enhance your versatility and strengthen your professional presence.
- **Be a can-do champion whenever you can** in your vertical, horizontal, and diagonal exchanges inside and outside your organization.
- **Keep adding career-enhancing items** to your can-do portfolio that demonstrate your can-do mindset and your STAR accomplishments.
- **And, never forget that all this works only if you:**
  - Follow the to do or not to do guidelines provided in the sit-do protocol, rather than just jumping in and doing whatever professional work you want to do.
  - Give your team members the opportunity to lead and star, rather than always trying to be the center of attention.
  - Always back your words with actions.
  - Give plenty of credit to others for successes, and assume your share of responsibility for setbacks.

THE CAN-DO LEADER'S LEXICON

A

ASPIRE: Acronym to help managers remember the key elements of a coaching process that gets desired results. ASPIRE stands for:

- Assess the situation.
- Specify the desired outcomes.
- Plan how they will be achieved.
- Initiate action.
- Review progress.
- Encourage appropriate adjustments.

It can also help you remember how to encourage continuous learning when delegating and coaching.

B

Bending the Iron Law of Managerial Delegation: Challenging the traditional notion that if you are not delegating you are not managing. Frees you up to become more successful as a leader and a professional. See also *both/and thinking, multi-impacting,* and *think TPL.*

Both/and Thinking: Contrary to the myth of the iron law of managerial delegation, the both/and mindset enables managers to let go of "either I'm leading or I'm doing" thinking, and recognize that being *both* a leader *and* a doer can be mutually reinforcing activities. See also *either/or thinking* and *multi-impacting.*

C

Can-Do Champions: Can-do leaders who develop a strong professional presence in their field and have considerable career security. They build their brand by continuing to demonstrate a can-do mindset that is backed by solid professional accomplishments in their employing organization and beyond. Can-do champions also encourage and inspire other player-managers to demonstrate versatility as both effective leaders and skilled professional specialists. See also *can-do networks, can-do spirit, can-do career portfolio,* and *career security.*

Can-Do Culture: A culture promoted by can-do champions that encourages team members to continually improve their ability to get the right things done. A "we-can-do" approach to team building that is the opposite of a boss-dependent culture. See also *can-do learning culture.*

Can-Do Leader Zone: A useful reminder of the fundamental people management responsibilities that all leaders inherit when they take on a management position. The three axes—task, people, and learning—remind us that, if you are going to be the sort of player-manager who excels at building teams that continue to improve their ability to get the right things done with high levels of skill and enthusiasm, these three dimensions will require your continuing attention as a leader. See also *can-do leader, can-do mind shift, think TPL,* and *power pause.*

Can-Do Leaders: Player-managers who succeed as both managers and professionals by letting go of conventional management thinking and selectively *doing* hands-on work in a way that advances their leadership agenda and enables them to continue to contribute their professional expertise. See also *can-do mind shift* and *can-do champion.*

Can-Do Leadership (CDL): A new leadership model for the increasingly knowledge-driven, cost-competitive 21st-century work world. Provides high-impact winning strategies for people in management who, in addition to having formal management responsibilities, find they also have to continue performing significant chunks of professional work that requires considerable technical-functional knowledge and skills. See also *can-do leader* and *can-do mind shift.*

Can-Do Learning Culture: A shared commitment to continuous learning that is promoted by can-do leaders when they are engaged in situational doing. Can-do leaders use their LENS (leadership effect never stops) to be a role model for creating the kind of learning culture that encourages everyone to be open to giving and receiving instructive on-the-spot performance feedback, positive negative feedback, sit-do coaching, and candid sit-do postmortem feedback sessions.

Can-Do Mind Shift: Letting go of conventional either/or thinking about leading and doing as a player-manager to become a can-do leader who makes use of the fact that leading and doing can be mutually reinforcing activities. See also *bending the iron law of managerial delegation, both/ and thinking, situational doing,* and *think TPL.*

Can-Do Networks: People with whom can-do leaders have mutually beneficial relationships for helping one another get things done. A far-reaching, multileveled can-do network can greatly enhance a can-do leader's professional reputation. See also *can-do champion* and *career security.*

Can-Do Spirit: The commitment, competence, and courage to get things done that is unleashed and powerfully sustained when a person's key VITALS talents and motivators are significantly engaged. See also *can-do spirit VITALS checkup.*

Can-Do Spirit VITALS Checkup: Assessment that helps people identify the key VITALS motivators that activate and sustain their can-do spirit. This assessment is included in appendix II.

Career Portfolio: A collection of documents and other artifacts that people can use to validate claims they make about themselves. Can-do leaders are well positioned to add items to their career portfolio that nicely demonstrate their can-do mindset and accomplishments. See also *can-do champion, career security,* and *STAR.*

Career Security: A measure of a person's employability. Your career security is the extent to which you would be able to get a job that you would like to have, if you were to lose your current job. Can-do leaders increase their career security by continually demonstrating their ability to add value both as managers and as professional contributors. See also *can-do champions.*

CDL: Can-do leader(ship).

CDL Advantage: Leadership and professional opportunities that can-do leaders have because they are positioned as both leaders and doers. See also *situational doing.*

CDL Playbook: A quick review of winning strategies for becoming a can-do leader.

CLEAR: An acronym that helps managers remember how to assign tasks in a way that very clearly specifies the responsibility, authority, and accountability associated with the work they are delegating. CLEAR stands for:

- Clarity: Clarify specific goals and parameters, and explain why the task was assigned.
- Linkages: Identify key task interdependencies.
- Expectations: Prioritize assignments and address any unusual features of the situation.
- Authority: Delegate sufficient authority and specify the degree of freedom in executing a task.
- Results: Discuss timeframe and precise form of deliverables.

E

Either/Or Thinking: The "either I'm leading or I'm doing" mindset associated with the myth of the iron law of managerial delegation. Inhibits managers' ability to see opportunities to address leadership issues while doing some of their team's work. See also *both/and thinking.*

EmPOWERSment: Term that refers to the true empowerment that occurs when the POWERS associated with can-do success are fully addressed. Use the POWERS acronym to remember the six different powers associated with a person becoming fully empowered to succeed. See also *POWERS.*

I

Individual Contributor (IC): A team member who does not have formal management responsibilities.

L

LENS: Acronym for the leadership effect never stops. Player-managers may try to act like colleagues when engaging in situational doing, but because of their power to evaluate, reward, and punish, they will inevitably be perceived as "the boss." Can-do leaders are always aware that, once they become a formal manager, they can never hide from the LENS through which their direct reports see them. Used effectively, the LENS can magnify the messages a leader wants to send.

M

Multi-Impacting: A time management, focus, and participation strategy that enhances performance. Instead of continually switching your attention back and forth between unrelated activities (traditional multitasking), engaging in an activity in a way that offers the promise of simultaneously achieving more than one desired objective. Can-do leaders often use this strategy to advance their leadership agenda when they are doing professional work with their team. See also *think TPL* and *situational doing.*

Myth of the Iron Law of Managerial Delegation: The misguided belief often promoted in management books, seminars, and courses that if you are not delegating you are not managing. See also *bending the iron law of managerial delegation.*

N

Natural First Move: A person's preference with regard to addressing task, people, and learning issues. Likely to be automatically activated if you do not take a power pause. See also *think TPL* and *TPL power pause.*

O

On-the-Spot Performance Feedback: Real-time feedback that gives people specific knowledge of the significant effects that their performance is having in defined areas that are primarily under their control. See also *can-do learning culture* and *positive-negative feedback.*

P

Player-Managers: Hands-on leaders who in addition to having formal management responsibilities also continue to perform significant chunks of professional work that requires considerable technical-functional knowledge and skills.

Positive-Negative Feedback: Corrective feedback that is communicated in a very positive way by emphasizing the significant improvement opportunities that can come with accepting and acting on this corrective feedback. See also *can-do learning culture.*

Power Pause: A mental routine that activates deliberative thinking when making important assessments and decisions. Power pauses reduce the mistakes that even experts make when thinking too fast. They also increase the range of relevant possibilities and options that are properly considered. See also *TPL power pauses* and *VITALS power pauses.*

POWERS: Acronym for proficiency, opportunity, willingness, encouragement, resources, and strategies. To fully empower their direct reports, can-do leaders focus on addressing these factors when delegating assignments. See also *emPOWERSment.*

S

Situational Doing (Sit-Do): Selectively doing professional work with teammates when, as a player-manager, it is situationally appropriate. Doing professional work for the right reasons positions can-do leaders to continue to make useful professional contributions. This also allows player-managers to get the kind of information they need to become better at delegating, addressing learning gaps, and leading their teams. See also *can-do mind shift* and *sit-do decision protocol.*

Sit-Do Coaching: In-depth coaching typically initiated by a can-do leader's situational doing observations. Also includes off-site coaching prompted by on-site performance observations, direct reports coaching one another, direct reports coaching their manager, or on-site coaching that reinforces off-site training. See also *can-do learning culture.*

Sit-Do Decision Protocol: Criteria that should be considered when player-managers are deciding whether to engage in situational doing. The sit-do decision protocol helps can-do leaders become mindful of what they need to know to make well-informed do-or-delegate decisions. See also *can-do mind shift.*

Sit-Do Postmortem Feedback Sessions: Feedback sessions modeled on the process used by Blue Angel elite navy flight teams, during which everyone who was involved in a sortie can openly provide candid feedback, regardless of rank. To promote candor and pinpoint accountability for needed improvements in team functioning, can-do leaders can use Blue Angel–style sit-do postmortem feedback sessions at the conclusion of significant phases of important assignments they have worked on with their team. See also *can-do learning culture.*

STAR: A well-known acronym that provides a useful structure for describing your can-do accomplishments:
- Situation: Any challenges, problems, or opportunities you addressed.
- Task: What you had to get done.
- Action(s): The key decisions and actions you and your team took.

- Results: What you ultimately were able to achieve with your team.

See also *can-do career portfolio* and *career security*.

T

Think TPL: A mantra that reminds can-do leaders to give appropriate attention to the relevant task, people, and learning issues. Thinking TPL can help you remember to do what needs to be done to lead your team into the can-do leader zone. Making a conscious effort to think TPL will reduce the possibility that you revert back to the narrow mindset of an individual contributor when you are engaged in situational doing. See also *natural first move, power pause, TPL,* and *TPL leadership style profiler.*

TPL (Task, People, Learning): Managers must address these dimensions of leadership with competence if they are to become can-do leaders who get things done in the present and prepare their people and teams for the future. The moment that individual contributors are assigned a management role or appointed to a management position, they take on the responsibility for anticipating and appropriately addressing the relevant task, people, and learning issues that are embedded in the things they do and the decisions they make. See also *can-do leader zone, natural first move, situational doing, TPL power pause,* and *TPL leadership style profiler.*

TPL Leadership Style Profiler: A questionnaire that helps you determine your natural first move for addressing task, people, and learning issues. The TPL leadership style profiler is in appendix I.

TP&L Power Pause: Adding & to the TPL power pause to remind you to focus on promoting a can-do learning culture and make sure you are giving particular attention to the learning dimension. See also *on-the-spot performance feedback, positive-negative feedback,* and *power pause.*

TPL Power Pause: Using the think TPL mantra to activate deliberative thinking with regard to considering the potential task, people, and learning issues that might need to be addressed when making an assessment prior to making a decision or taking a particular action. See also *natural first move* and *power pause.*

V

VITALS: Acronym that stands for values, interests, talents, ambitions, longings, and styles; the true source of each person's can-do spirit. See also *VITALS power pause.*

VITALS Power Pause: Using the VITALS acronym as a mental checklist to make sure that you're giving full consideration to the impact that a person's VITALS profile may have on the outcome of a decision you are making. A routine that reminds you to engage in deliberate thinking when making assessments of VITALS profiles. See also *power pause.*

APPENDIX I:
CAN-DO LEADER TPL
LEADERSHIP STYLE PROFILER

This profiler will help you gain insight into your natural leadership style. It is important that you give candid responses.

You are not being tested for "right" and "wrong" answers. Don't spend too much time thinking about each situation. When choosing your response, your immediate reaction is probably the real you.

Start at the beginning. Do not read what is on the next page until you have completed the page in front of you. Skipping ahead might bias your responses and give you a false reading of your leadership style.

Completing the entire profiler, parts 1, 2, and 3, should not take more than 15 minutes.

Can-Do Leader TPL Leadership Style Profiler: Part 1

For each of the following questions, rank your responses 1, 2, or 3, according to your preferences.

- Choose 1 for the response that is most like you.
- Choose 2 for your second choice.
- Choose 3 for the response that is least like you.

Sample question:

Rank		For sports, I'd rather:
3	A	Watch on television.
1	B	Play on a team.
2	C	Play with a friend.

1. When delegating a task, I focus on:

	A	Planning, setting goals, and monitoring performance.
	B	Using a personal communication style that direct reports will respond to favorably.
	C	Identifying areas where my direct reports may need further training if they are to perform this task successfully.

2. When discussing an issue with direct reports, I like to:

	A	Keep the conversation focused on coming to an understanding of how this issue will be resolved.
	B	Try to understand what the other people are feeling, rather than just listening to their words.
	C	Ask questions that will inspire them to think about this issue in ways they may not have considered before.

3. I facilitate decision making by:

	A	Making sure that a careful analysis is made of both the facts and the desired outcomes, so that the best choice can be made.
	B	Listening to others and then finding the solution that generates the most support.
	C	Encouraging people to consider points of view that may differ from their initial way of analyzing the situation.

4. If an employee is chronically late, I:

	A	Without hesitation, tell the person that tardiness is unacceptable.
	B	Ask the person to give the reason(s) why this tardiness is occurring, so that I can understand the problem from his or her point of view.
	C	Make the person aware of the impact of his or her tardiness.

5. For each of my direct reports, I like to focus on:

	A	Getting the things done that must get done.
	B	Understanding their career aspirations, so that, whenever possible, I can assign tasks that they will find highly motivating.
	C	Developing the skills that will enable them to excel at important tasks.

6. As a role model, I:

	A	Put pressure on myself to demonstrate a high level of task performance so that others will be inspired to meet a high standard when performing their assigned tasks.
	B	Strive to demonstrate the kind of sensitivity to people's needs that builds effective work relationships, and hope that my direct reports will be inspired to do the same.
	C	Am continually broadening my skill base, and hope that this inspires others to do the same.

7. When giving feedback, I:

	A	Praise performance that exceeds goals that have been set, and I make sure to point out assigned tasks that were not completed successfully.
	B	Always keep in mind the feelings of the person receiving the feedback.
	C	Focus on behaviors and their consequences so the best behaviors get reinforced and the least desirable behaviors gradually change.

Please proceed to part 2.

Can-Do Leader TPL Leadership Style Profiler: Part 2

Read the mini-case and answer the questions. For each of the following questions, rank your responses as 1, 2, or 3, according to your preferences. Again please remember: There are no "right" or "wrong" answers, just your answers.

You have assigned Chris, a direct report, the task of creating a computer-generated cash flow report for management that will accurately state the firm's cash position on a daily basis. The firm is highly leveraged so having a timely report is very important to managing the firm's debt. Management is very eager to have this report, and Chris is going to give you an update on the report's progress. You are looking forward to meeting with Chris because he has a history of getting the job done. At most, you may have to make a few minor suggestions to keep Chris on track to success.

Keeping the upcoming meeting with Chris in mind, please rank your responses to each of the following questions.

When answering these questions, you could also think about a similar situation at work or school where you are directing the work of someone in whom you have great confidence. The key is to give responses that reflect how you are likely to behave when you are managing someone and you believe things are going well.

Remember, in this situation you are having a good day!

1. When discussing the approaching deadline for this project with Chris, I will focus on:

	A	Planning, setting goals, and monitoring performance.
	B	Using a communication style that puts him at ease, and makes him receptive to what I have to say.
	C	Identifying areas where he might need further training if he is to perform this task successfully.

2. When discussing work issues with Chris, I will:

	A	Keep the conversation focused on coming to an understanding of how each issue will be resolved.
	B	Try to understand what he is feeling, rather than just listening to his words.
	C	Ask questions that will inspire him to think about these issues in new ways.

3. When Chris needs help, I encourage problem solving by:

	A	Being sure that a careful analysis is made of both the facts and the desired outcomes, so that the best choice can be made.
	B	Listening to his thoughts and then finding a solution that we can both support.
	C	Encouraging him to consider points of view that may differ from his initial way of analyzing the situation.

4. Because this project is very visible, I will focus on:

	A	Making sure that Chris does the things that must get done.
	B	Making sure that Chris continues to find this project motivating, and, if necessary, make appropriate adjustments in the incentives he is offered for completing the job successfully.
	C	Making sure that Chris develops the skills that will enable him to excel at this task.

5. When I assigned this project, I:

	A	Identified and clearly communicated objectives and set meaningful deadlines.
	B	Discussed this project with Chris prior to assigning it, so that I could be sure he had the appropriate motivation.
	C	Determined Chris's strengths and weaknesses, and arranged for him to get help in developing the key skills he needs to complete the job successfully.

6. As a role model, I:

	A	Put pressure on myself to demonstrate a high level of task performance so that Chris and others will be inspired to meet a high standard when performing their assigned tasks.
	B	Strive to demonstrate sensitivity to Chris's needs so that he is encouraged to participate in an effective working relationship with me.
	C	Am continually broadening my skill base, and hope that this inspires Chris to do the same.

7. When giving Chris feedback, I:

	A	Praise performance that exceeds goals that have been set, and I make sure to point out assigned tasks that were not completed successfully.
	B	Always keep his feelings in mind while I am giving him feedback.
	C	Focus on his behaviors and their consequences, so the best behaviors get reinforced and the least desirable behaviors gradually change.

Please proceed to Part 3.

Can-Do Leader TPL Leadership Style Profiler: Part 3

Read the mini-case and answer the questions. For each of the following questions, rank your responses as 1, 2, or 3, according to your preferences. Again, please remember that there are no "right" or "wrong" answers, just your answers.

This time, let's assume that Chris has blown the deadline because he waited too long to tell you about his lack of technical knowledge about preparing a cash flow analysis. Chris is strong with computers, but doesn't understand accounting well enough to put all the pieces together. Your boss is very upset the report isn't ready but you still have time to pull it off, as long as you have a successful meeting with Chris and delegate some of his responsibilities to another analyst. You are feeling stressed because management is pressuring you to deliver, and you know that Chris, one of your best performers, will not be eager to let go of the project.

Keeping the upcoming meeting with Chris in mind, rank your responses to each of the following questions.

When answering these questions, you could also think about a similar situation at work or school where you are directing the work of someone who is not getting the job done as well as you had hoped. The key is to give responses that reflect how you are likely to behave when you are managing someone and you believe things are not going well.

Remember, in this situation you are having a bad day!

1. When discussing the missed deadline with Chris, I will focus on:

	A	Planning, setting goals, and monitoring performance.
	B	Using a communication style that puts him at ease, and makes him receptive to what I have to say.
	C	Identifying the areas where he will need further training if he is to get the project done successfully, and then arrange for this training.

2. When I meet with Chris, I:

	A	Keep the conversation focused on coming to an understanding of how each issue will be resolved so we can make up for the missed deadline.
	B	Try to understand what he is feeling as we discuss what to do about the missed deadline, rather than just listening to his words.
	C	Ask questions that will inspire him to think about why he missed the deadline and what can be done to correct the situation.

3. In the areas where Chris needs help, I will facilitate problem solving by:

	A	Being sure that a careful analysis is made of both the facts and the desired outcomes so the best choice can be made.
	B	Listening to his thoughts and then finding a solution that we can both support.
	C	Encouraging him to consider points of view that may differ from his initial way of analyzing the situation.

4. Because this project is very visible, I will focus on:

	A	Making sure Chris does the things that must get done.
	B	Making sure Chris continues to find the project motivating, and, if necessary, make appropriate adjustments in the incentives he is offered for completing this job successfully.
	C	Making sure that Chris develops the skills that will enable him to excel at this task.

5. Looking back, I realize that when I assigned this project, I should have done a better job of:

	A	Identifying and clearly communicating the objectives, and setting meaningful deadlines.
	B	Discussing this job with Chris prior to assigning it, so that I was sure he had the appropriate motivation.
	C	Determining Chris's strengths and weaknesses, and arranging for him to get help developing the key skills he needed to complete the project successfully.

6. As a role model, I must now:

	A	Put pressure on myself to demonstrate a high level of task performance so that Chris and others will be inspired to do the same in completing this project.
	B	Strive to demonstrate sensitivity to Chris's needs so that he is well motivated to complete this project successfully.
	C	Continue to broaden my skill base so that Chris is inspired to learn the new skills he must master to successfully this project.

7. When giving Chris feedback, I will:

	A	Be focusing on assessing where we are with respect to completing the task.
	B	Always keep in mind his feelings.
	C	Focus on his behaviors and their consequences, so that the best behaviors get reinforced and the least desirable behaviors gradually change.

Congratulations! You have completed the profiler. Please review the example on the next page and then proceed to Can-Do Leader TPL leadership style scoring sheet on the next page.

Example Only: Do Not Fill in Here

Can-Do Leader TPL Leadership Style Scoring

Instructions:

1. Copy your scores from each part into the rows of Table 1.
2. Add the scores by summing the columns.
3. Graph each part in Table 2 by shading upward to your score.

Table 1

	Part 1				Part 2				Part 3		
	A	B	C		A	B	C		A	B	C
1	1	3	2	1	3	1	2	1	3	2	1
2	2	3	1	2	3	1	2	2	3	2	1
3	1	3	2	3	2	1	3	3	2	3	1
4	2	3	1	4	3	2	1	4	3	1	2
5	1	2	3	5	3	2	1	5	3	1	2
6	2	3	1	6	1	2	3	6	1	3	2
7	1	2	3	7	3	1	2	7	3	2	1

Sum	10	19	13		18	10	14		18	14	10

Table 2

Example Can-Do Leader TPL Leadership Style Profiles

	Part 1: Neutral			Part 2: Positive Experience			Part 3: Negative Experience		
	A	B	C	A	B	C	A	B	C
1									
2									
3									
4									
5									
6									
7									
8									
9									
10	▓				▓				▓
11	▓				▓				▓
12	▓				▓				▓
13	▓		▓		▓				▓
14	▓		▓		▓	▓		▓	▓
15	▓		▓		▓	▓		▓	▓
16	▓		▓		▓	▓		▓	▓
17	▓		▓		▓	▓		▓	▓
18	▓		▓	▓	▓	▓	▓	▓	▓
19	▓	▓	▓	▓	▓	▓	▓	▓	▓
20	▓	▓	▓	▓	▓	▓	▓	▓	▓
21	▓	▓	▓	▓	▓	▓	▓	▓	▓
	Task	People	Learning	Task	People	Learning	Task	People	Learning

Can-Do Leader TPL Leadership Style Scoring

Instructions:

1. Copy your scores from each part into the rows of Table 1.
2. Add the scores by summing the columns.
3. Graph each part in Table 2 by shading upward to your score.

Table 1

	Part 1				Part 2				Part 3		
	A	**B**	**C**		**A**	**B**	**C**		**A**	**B**	**C**
1				**1**				**1**			
2				**2**				**2**			
3				**3**				**3**			
4				**4**				**4**			
5				**5**				**5**			
6				**6**				**6**			
7				**7**				**7**			

Sum

Table 2

Your Can-Do Leader TPL Leadership Style Profile

	Part 1: Neutral			Part 2: Positive Experience			Part 3: Negative Experience		
	A	B	C	A	B	C	A	B	C
1									
2									
3									
4									
5									
6									
7									
8									
9									
10									
11									
12									
13									
14									
15									
16									
17									
18									
19									
20									
21									
	Task	People	Learning	Task	People	Learning	Task	People	Learning

Interpreting Your Profiler Scores

Please note: So as not to bias your responses, please do not read the following explanation of TPL scores until you have completed the can-do leader TPL leadership style profiler.

What Your TPL Scores Measure

The profiler measures your likely preference for focusing on task, people, or learning issues when you are in the role of manager.

- Part 1 of the profiler indicates the relative importance you attach to task, people, and learning issues when you are managing someone and are not feeling any strong emotions about what is happening.
- Part 2 measures the order of priority you give to task, people, and learning issues when you believe things are going well. These are your TPL tendencies when you are feeling good and not under stress.
- Part 3 measures the order of priority you give task, people, and learning issues when you are in a management situation that is stressful for you.

To better understand how this scoring system works, let's take an example. If your bar for task is the tallest in Part 1, this suggests that when you are not feeling any strong positive or negative emotions, your natural preference is to give top priority to task issues before attending to people or learning issues.

However, your tallest bar in Part 2 might be people. If so, this suggests that when you are feeling good about a management situation, your natural tendency is to focus on people issues—being supportive and attentive to individual needs. This is the people side of management.

Continuing to Part 3, here your priorities may shift again, and your tallest bar is learning. This suggests that under stress you are likely to put the greatest emphasis on making sure your direct reports learn what you believe they need to learn to accomplish a given objective.

Of course, the above hypothetical example is only one of many possible patterns that have been recorded. In your case, there may be minor shifts in the level of commitment you give to task, people, and learning issues, but no change in the relative priority that you give them. Or, it could be that everything simply stays the same.

By taking a moment to study your TPL profile for each emotional context, you can get a good idea of what you believe your natural preferences for attending to task, people, and learning issues are at this point in your management career.

This profiler is based on self-perceptions. However, how you see yourself may be very different from how others see you. Accurate data on the impact you are having on other people with regard to task, people, and learning issues can be generated by getting feedback from real-life situations or role plays.

The relevance of task, people, and learning issues for leadership and the importance of understanding your natural leadership style are explained in chapter 2.

APPENDIX II:
CAN-DO SPIRIT VITALS
CHECKUP

Here's a simple strategy you can use to identify the kinds of tasks and projects that will help you develop a can-do spirit at work.

1. Think of two or three projects or activities you have participated in over the past five years that really turned you on. Not just at work but in any aspect of your life.
2. Think of two or three projects or activities you've tried that really turned you off.

To better understand why you found these activities highly energizing or very demotivating, try reflecting on them as you answer the following questions. Your answers will give you insights into the VITALS that are important to you.

Values are the standards or principles you believe are important to uphold in life, which could include trustworthiness, service to others, loyalty, fairness, personally important cultural dictates, and other deeply held beliefs.

- Were the kinds of things you were supposed to do in sync with your personal **values**?
  - I felt like I was strongly supporting things I really believe in (green).
  - This project did not significantly involve any of my important values (yellow).
  - I was asked to do something that would violate my personal code (red).

- Give some examples of specific things about this activity that would explain your green, yellow, or red rating.

Interests are work-related subject areas that grab and hold your attention.
- Did you find any significant aspects of this activity **interesting** and engaging?
  - This is an area I would enjoy learning a lot more about (green).
  - This is not an area I find particularly interesting (yellow).
  - I found this project really boring (red).
- Give some examples of specific things about this activity that would explain your green, yellow, or red rating.

Talents refer to strong skills you have developed, as well as the underlying ability or aptitude that makes it possible for you to develop a noteworthy skill.
- Did this project give you opportunities to develop and deploy skills in areas where you have a **talent** that would be fun to continue developing?
  - I believe I was tapping into a talent that I would enjoy continuing to develop and use (green).
  - I could get better at doing this sort of thing, but it's not a skill area that I have any interest in developing (yellow).
  - I think I have very little talent for some of the things I was supposed to do, and there's very little chance I could ever get much better at them (red).
- Give some examples of specific things about this activity that would explain your green, yellow, or red rating.

Ambitions are the goals you have for your career and personal life—what you want to be and achieve, both on the job and when not at work. They may also reflect your financial goals.
- Did this project get you closer to realizing your career **ambitions**?

- ○ It seemed like I was doing some things that would prepare me for the career I want to pursue (green).
- ○ What I was doing didn't seem particularly relevant, given my current career ambitions (yellow).
- ○ It seemed like I was taking a step backward, given the direction I want to go in my career (red).
- Give some examples of specific things about this activity that would explain your green, yellow, or red rating.

Longings are the nagging (when not sufficiently satisfied) psychological needs you bring to the workplace, such as the need for achievement, affiliation, power, and autonomy, as well as the desire for stability and predictability. Some people also hope to satisfy the need for adventure and creativity at work.

- Did the role you played in this project allow you to satisfy some of your strongest psychological needs and **longings**?
  - ○ The work I was able to do during this project was psychologically very rewarding (green).
  - ○ The kind of work I was supposed to do during this project didn't seem particularly rewarding (yellow).
  - ○ I found it hard to concentrate on what I was supposed to be doing because I long to do a very different kind of work (red).
- Give some examples of specific things about this activity that would explain your green, yellow, or red rating.

Style refers to how you characteristically take in information, make decisions, deal with success and failure, and interact with others. The style concept focuses on your preferences rather than your abilities. When you understand other people's personal styles, you are better able to find effective ways of influencing them.

- Did the organizational culture associated with doing this activity suit your personal **style** and allow you to feel comfortable being the kind of person you really are?

- ∘ I felt fully accepted being the real me (green).
- ∘ I believe I was expected to behave in ways that didn't always suit my temperament (yellow).
- ∘ I didn't feel at all comfortable being the person I really am in this culture (red).
- • Give some examples of specific things about this activity that would explain your green, yellow, or red rating.

Using the above VITALS checkup to reflect on past, current, and future activities will help you identify the most powerful personal motivators and demotivators that make up your motivational profile.

REFERENCES

Drucker, P. 2008. *The Essential Drucker: The Best of Sixty Years of Peter Drucker's Essential Writings on Management.* (Collins Business Essentials Series). New York: HarperCollins.

Franklin, B. 2003. *The Autobiography of Benjamin Franklin.* New Haven, CT: Yale Nota Bene Book.

Gladwell, M. 2005. *Blink: The Power of Thinking Without Thinking.* New York: Little, Brown.

Kahneman, D. 2011. *Thinking, Fast and Slow.* New York: Farrar, Straus, and Giroux.

McClelland, D.C. 1988. *Human Motivation.* New York: Cambridge University Press.

Satterthwaite, F., and G. D'Orsi. 2003. *The Career Portfolio Workbook: Using the Newest Tool in Your Job-Hunting Arsenal to Impress Employers and Land a Great Job.* New York: McGraw-Hill.

ABOUT THE AUTHORS

Frank Satterthwaite is a professor of organizational leadership and past director of the MBA program at Johnson & Wales University. He is the senior author of *The Career Portfolio Workbook: Using the Newest Tool in Your Job-Hunting Arsenal to Impress Employers and Land a Great Job* (McGraw-Hill 2003), which was selected as an Editor's Choice at the *Wall Street Journal's* CareerJournal.com. His autobiography as an athlete, *The Three-Wall Nick and Other Angles* (Holt 1979), received critical acclaim from *The New Yorker* magazine.

Frank has given numerous presentations with Jamie Millard on developing the can-do mindset at international conferences, and has been a frequent blogger for the Association for Talent Development (ATD) Management Community of Practice. Frank and Jamie's webcasts, podcasts, and video clips on can-do leadership are included in the ATD online library.

In addition to Frank and Jamie's cover story for *TD* magazine in June 2016, Frank's articles have appeared in numerous national magazines, including *Esquire*, and he has appeared on nationally broadcast radio and TV programs in both the United States and Canada. He also wrote and hosted six half-hour educational TV shows for PBS affiliate WXXI.

Frank has a management consulting and executive coaching practice in which he helps managers become can-do leaders. He studied psychology at Princeton and received a PhD in organizational behavior from Yale. He was also a member of the U.S. national men's squash team. Frank and his architect wife, Martha Werenfels, live in Rhode Island. They have (and are very proud of) two sons, Peter and Toby. Frank can be reached at franksatterthwaite@gmail.com.

Jamie Millard is the executive partner and co-founder of Lexington Leadership Partners, a leadership development firm focused on customized leadership training and executive coaching. Many of the book's can-do leader concepts were tested and refined based on his extensive experience as a leader, consultant, trainer, and coach.

Jamie's clients have included AECOM, AT&T, Bayer MaterialScience, Conti, Draper Laboratory, DuPont, EMC, GE, GTech, Heidrick & Stuggles, The Home Depot, IBM, KVH, The Learning Company, Macronix, Mercy Hospital, Mott MacDonald, Nationwide Insurance, Nuance, PwC, Raytheon, Rockwell Collins, Rohm & Haas, Schering Plough, State Street, United Technologies, U.S. Navy, VCE, and WEA Trust.

Jamie formerly led the National Organization Change Management Practice at CSC Consulting. Prior to that he was a managing director at Coopers & Lybrand (now PwC), which acquired Harbridge House, where he led the Continuous Improvement and Project Management practices. Earlier, he was a manager in Peat, Marwick, Mitchell & Co (now KPMG). He began his journey in leadership as a U.S. Army captain and U.S. Army Ranger.

Jamie and Frank regularly present at ATD and other international conferences on helping busy managers become can-do leaders. Together, they are featured in ATD webcasts, video clips, podcasts, and blogs, which are available in the ATD online library.

Jamie holds a BS from the U.S. Military Academy at West Point and an MBA from the University of Rhode Island. He is a member of the Global Educator Network with Duke Corporate Education, a professor at Hult International Business School, and an adjunct executive professor at Northeastern University. Jamie and his wife, Ann, live in Rhode Island, where they raised their three sons, Eric, Scott, and Adam. Jamie can be reached at jmillard@lexlead.com.

INDEX

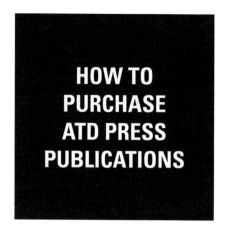

HOW TO PURCHASE ATD PRESS PUBLICATIONS

ATD Press publications are available worldwide in print and electronic format.

To place an order, please visit our online store: www.td.org/books.

Our publications are also available at select online and brick-and-mortar retailers.

Outside the United States, English-language ATD Press titles may be purchased through the following distributors:

United Kingdom, Continental Europe, the Middle East, North Africa, Central Asia, Australia, New Zealand, and Latin America
Eurospan Group
Phone: 44.1767.604.972
Fax: 44.1767.601.640
Email: eurospan@turpin-distribution.com
Website: www.eurospanbookstore.com

Asia
Cengage Learning Asia Pte. Ltd.
Phone: (65)6410-1200
Email: asia.info@cengage.com
Website: www.cengageasia.com

Nigeria
Paradise Bookshops
Phone: 08033075133
Email: paradisebookshops@gmail.com
Website: www.paradisebookshops.com

South Africa
Knowledge Resources
Phone: +27 (11) 706.6009
Fax: +27 (11) 706.1127
Email: sharon@knowres.co.za
Web: www.kr.co.za

For all other territories, customers may place their orders at the ATD online store: **www.td.org/books**.